Making and managing
a trout lake

The lake built by the author near Pontesbury, Shropshire, U K

Making and managing a trout lake

Rupert Barrington

Fishing News Books Ltd
Farnham · Surrey · England

©Rupert Barrington 1983

British Library CIP Data

Barrington, Rupert
  Making and managing a trout lake
  1. Trout   2. Fish culture
  I. Title
  639.3′75′5   SH167.T86

ISBN 0 85238 126 3

Typeset by
Alresford Phototypesetting
Alresford, Hants

Printed in Great Britain by
Page Bros (Norwich) Ltd

Contents

Figures

Acknowledgement

I gratefully acknowledge the very useful advice and help given to me by my son John N Barrington BSc (Hons) a fish-farmer of considerable experience, who also took all the photographs included in the text.

Preface

As children, most of us were fascinated by water. We had to walk through every puddle we could find and many happy hours were spent on the beach making dams or channels with sea water or paddling in the local stream. As adults, we rarely lose that innate attraction to water and our holidays are invariably spent very close to it. Where possible we introduce it into our gardens even if it is only a goldfish pond. There is little doubt that the sight of open stretches of water has a relaxing and beneficial effect on most of us. Constable, Turner, Vermeer and many other great landscape artists knew this and made it the key subject in a large number of their best paintings.

Many of us would like to be able to look out over a lake from our house, but such an ambition can be achieved by very few. There are, however, some property owners or farmers who have a natural source of water on their land who could, if conditions were right, build a lake or large pond for themselves. It would seem a pity that anyone who has such material resources on their land should not make the best possible use of them, either for leisure purposes for which there will be an ever increasing demand or purely and simply for the satisfaction of creating a living piece of environment of an enduring character and something which will be an added attraction to the surrounding countryside.

Apart from its pleasing appearance, a lake could be a sound investment from several points of view. If properly planned it should improve the general environment, thereby adding a value to a property in excess of the actual cost of its construction. If the owner wishes, he can let the fishing rights for trout fishing only or for coarse fishing for which there is always a big demand. In times of drought, it could provide a vital supply of water for crop irrigation or horticulture. In countries where drought is common and prolonged, a lake or reservoir would not only be labour-

9

saving but life-saving for cattle or sheep. A lake can also form the nucleus of a shoot, with certain modifications, and this can be a very profitable sideline. In contrast, it could form an excellent conservation area mainly for birds, though it would be necessary to plant the trees and shrubs which are most likely to attract them.

The purpose of this small book is to give a fairly detailed account of what is involved in building and managing such a lake with special emphasis on trout fishing. The various difficulties and snags which can arise and the best way to overcome them are described. The book is based on the author's experience of building a lake in Shropshire which was about 2.2 acres (0.9 hectare) in area, with a capacity of some 17,000m³ (approximately 3.75 million gallons). By some standards this is small but it is large enough to hold a good stock of trout and be managed by one person.

The building of a dam to impound water is a more complicated procedure than it would at first appear and the work must be carefully carried out from the start. If a dam breaks, it usually does so without warning and there is very little that can be done to stop the escape of water. The damage caused by flooding from a burst dam can be enormous and the cost of repairing the break in the dam very high. The actual work of dam building has therefore been described in some detail with particular emphasis on the installation of the outflow system which is the key to efficient functioning of a lake. The same principles of engineering would apply in the construction of larger lakes.

It is not always necessary to build a dam. For example, in low-lying districts it may be possible simply to excavate out the site of a proposed lake or even a garden pool, obtaining the water supply from an existing stream or by abstracting it from a nearby stream. But in more hilly districts, where the site of the proposed lake lies in a natural valley with a stream running through it, a dam will almost certainly be necessary.

For the sake of completeness, two other types of outflow systems have been described.

Lake management is largely a matter of common sense; however, there are quite a number of snags and minor problems that might occur from time to time and the owner should be able to forestall these if he is aware that they could happen. Provided the dam is well built and the overflow system is in proper working order, there are very few difficulties which cannot be overcome.

Whoever owns a well-stocked trout lake in a populated area will soon receive many requests for the fishing rights. Careful thought should be given to such requests before taking on such a responsibility. Although the financial return may appear to be very attractive, the owner will be involved in a good deal of work which at first may not seem very sizable but will soon be very time consuming. If financial conditions permit, it is probably better to keep the fishing of a small trout lake on a private basis. There is no better way of entertaining friends and keeping them occupied than to allow them to fish a well-stocked lake, and if the owner is a keen angler he can choose the most favourable times for fishing and do so undisturbed in pleasant surroundings.

Against this must be set the necessity to shoulder the whole responsibility of protecting the property from poachers of all kinds – some human and others, furred or feathered. It is difficult and costly either to maintain a continuous watch, or to accept the losses which can easily follow if the water is left unattended for any great length of time. Properly authorized 'paying guests' are perhaps the most cost effective method of keeping away unwelcome intruders.

The reader will find frequent references to Water Authorities which are, of course, duly relevant to England and Wales, but in other parts of the world the appropriate authority may well be under a different name. Regulations may vary considerably from one country to another. In general, the more densely populated a country is, the stricter will be the regulations about the impounding of water by private persons and the avoidance of pollution and fish disease. In some countries where the population is widely scattered, there are few or no regulations and even if there were, it would be impossible and very costly to enforce them.

1
Water and soil requirements

When building a trout lake, several factors have to be considered, quite apart from the cost, and before work starts each of these must be carefully examined. The three most important things to investigate are the quality and quantity of the water supply and the type of subsoil likely to be found at the proposed site. If, for example, the subsoil proves to be very deficient in clay, it might be worth considering the use of plastic lining, about which more will be said later.

Quality of water
A badly polluted stream is obvious to the naked eye, the water being dull and smokey in colour and the bottom covered with a brown–green slime, with a complete absence of any healthy looking water weed or any aquatic life, except perhaps tubifex worms which can tolerate heavy pollution. This unpleasant state is usually caused by an excess of nitrogen and phosphate which uses up the natural oxygen in the water; until such pollution has been removed, it could not be used as a water supply for a trout lake.

If, on the other hand, a stream contains an abundance of aquatic life, with plenty of healthy water weed, it would almost certainly be unpolluted and suitable for trout, but a chemical analysis of the water nevertheless should be carried out to exclude certain mineral contaminants.

In hilly districts, there are often natural springs that keep up a steady flow throughout the year. The only pollution in such water might be minerals. If the surrounding soil is peaty, the water may be too acid for trout but this can sometimes be remedied by the addition of alkalis, as will be described later. A natural spring, with good quality water, makes a perfect water supply for a trout lake: there is no risk of pollution and

13

the cool temperature of the water is ideal for trout.

When water is taken from a main river, as is the case with many trout lakes today, there is always the risk that the quality of the water may deteriorate temporarily as the result of pollution or fish disease upstream. For example, if there are several fish farms using the water of one river, each farm being allowed to discharge back a limited percentage of its toxic effluent, there is a risk that the total percentage may build up sufficiently to have toxic effects on the aquatic life downstream.

In all cases the water must be tested by a Public Health Laboratory for such contents as lead, copper, iron and magnesium, all of which may be present in minute but harmless quantities. Tests are made for total hardness and undesirable pollutants but, most important of all, for acidity or alkalinity, in other words, the pH; this is of considerable importance to all freshwater fish. Acid waters have a pH value of less than 7.0, which is the neutral point. Alkaline waters have a pH greater than 7.0. A hard water is alkaline and contains much calcium carbonate and bicarbonate.

A stable pH of about 7.25 is suitable for trout and other forms of aquatic life. Stability is important and the more alkaline the water, the the more stable the pH. Sudden variations, such as may be caused by heavy thaws or torrential rain, may result in a sudden drop in pH to below 5.0 at which stage trout will begin to die.

When the water is very acid, it can be rendered more alkaline by spreading ground lime or calcium oxide on the bottom of the lake at a rate of about 2 tonnes per hectare (2.5 acres) if the pH is 4, and 1 tonne per hectare if the pH is 6 (Huet). The liming must, of course, be done before the lake is filled.

As mentioned already, one of the main pollutants of small rivers in the countryside is excessive nitrogen which removes oxygen from the water and thus kills all aquatic life. The effluent from slurry ponds or silage pits and excess fertilizers will cause such pollution, if they seep into rivers. Herbicides, if used on vegetation near a river, without the necessary precautions, will have a similar toxic effect. Diesel oil, domestic fuel or waste oil will destroy every form of aquatic life if it gets into a stream in any quantity.

Brackish water, with salinity of about 25%, must be mentioned because both rainbow and brown trout grow rapidly in it after introduction as two-year-old fish. The so-called 'slob' trout lives naturally in such water. It is mainly a bottom feeding fish and so is of no great interest to

14

the trout angler. Estuary water is now being used more and more by fish farmers, both because of its good growing qualities and the increasing shortage of suitable inland waters.

Quantity of water

A spring which never dries up and has water of good quality is the ideal water supply for a lake and, even if it stops flowing during times of drought, use can be made of it provided the capacity of the lake is large enough to withstand a drop of about 0.5m in its level. Large volumes of static water, if exposed to the sun and wind, will be quite suitable for

Fig 1   An ideal supply stream and spawning bed

15

trout if there is a deep, and therefore cool, part of the lake where trout can congregate during very hot weather. For example, the levels of reservoirs containing large stocks of trout often drop a metre or more during long periods of drought, with their feeder streams virtually dried up, but the trout invariably survive.

Small streams and large ditches having running water for perhaps only nine months of the year will often be quite sufficient to supply a lake that has an impervious subsoil. Several small ditches draining pasture land which have a good flow of water during most of the year, can be piped to a central point and provide sufficient water to keep a lake well filled. This method was used by the author and proved to be entirely satisfactory. The lake contained about 150 rainbow trout. During a long drought the water level dropped by 0.5m with no serious effect on the fish. It would probably be unwise to use water from ditches draining agricultural land, where there is almost always a high annual application of nitrogenous fertilizer.

Marsh ground, with no visible sign of a stream, often covers a watercourse which has become completely silted up and overgrown with rushes and weed over the years (*Figs 2* and *3*). Such a site might well be excavated and become much more useful as a lake than as a grazing pasture.

If there is no source of water on the site where it is proposed to build a lake, but there is a river nearby, it is sometimes possible to obtain permission to abstract water from the mainstream and to return it, via the lake, to the stream lower down (*Figs 4* and *5*). Abstraction of water from a mainstream also has the distinct advantage that the construction costs would be less, because in low-lying country where there are few natural dips in the ground it would be possible, instead of building a dam, merely to construct an embankment round the margins of the site, excavating from the centre. The chief expense would be laying the supply pipe from the mainstream to the lake and the outflow pipe from the lake back to the mainstream. Taking water in this way from a mainstream has the advantage that during times of heavy rain, when the river may rise 1m or so, the water entering the lake can be controlled by a sluice, thus avoiding all the ill effects of a flood, such as excessive silt and the many impurities contained in surface drainage.

Sinking a borehole is initially expensive and will involve using an electric pump and laying on an electricity supply. The pump would need to work long enough each day to keep the water level steady. The

Fig 2 A good site for a small lake. An existing stream (not visible) runs through it

Fig 3 Another good site. The stream running through it is concealed by bog

expense of this could be offset by the use of water for other purposes such as for irrigation or stock farming. Such a source would guarantee a continuous supply of high-quality water without risk of outside contamination, the only real disadvantage being the possibility of electrical power cuts, but these may be overcome by using auxiliary generators.

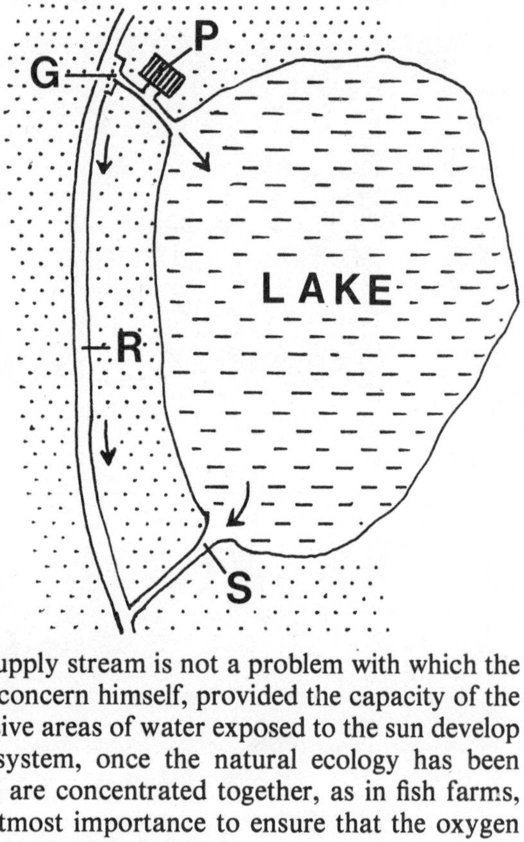

Fig 4 Abstraction of water from a main stream on fairly level ground
G – abstraction point with grid or sluice
P – pump, but gravity feed may be possible
R – main stream
S – outflow to main stream

The rate of flow of the supply stream is not a problem with which the owner of a trout lake need concern himself, provided the capacity of the lake is large enough. Extensive areas of water exposed to the sun develop their own waste-disposal system, once the natural ecology has been established. But where fish are concentrated together, as in fish farms, the rate of flow is of the utmost importance to ensure that the oxygen content of the water is sufficiently high for trout.

Type of subsoil
It is essential to find out what sort of subsoil is likely to be found at the bottom of the proposed lake site and this can be done either by excavating a deep test-hole or by taking samples with boreholes in various places. This method will give a very good indication of what will be

Fig 5   Abstraction of water from mainstream through a grid by gravity only

found at greater depths, but if the site lies in a natural dip in the land, it will not be necessary to take samples at a depth of more than 1m.

If the soil samples have a clay content of 30% or more, mixed with sand, conditions for lake building would be ideal, and there should be no leaks either in the dam or lake bottom. If the clay content is considerably less than 30% and is mixed with a high proportion of sand, it becomes necessary to bring in clay from elsewhere to construct a central core for the dam as shown in *Fig 6*. The top of the clay core must be above water level and the base must be dug well below the level of the lake bottom.

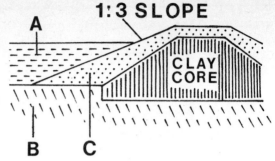

Fig 6 Cross section of dam with central core of soil of over 30% clay content
A – water in lake
B – subsoil
C – local soil with less than 30% clay

The local sand and clay subsoil can be used to build up the rest of the dam. The slope of the dam on the lakeside should be not less than 1 in 3 to lessen the chances of erosion by wave action. A slope of 1 in 4 is recommended by Behrendt.

Sometimes the subsoil will be found to be almost pure clay and this may, of course, be used for building a dam; in wet weather, however, it would be much more difficult to work. Pure clay should not be allowed to dry out because permanent cracks may form on the dam and these could give rise to leaks. To prevent this, the surface of the dam should be covered with top soil as soon as it has been completed. Pure clay often contains large flint stones and as many of these as possible should be removed because water tends to seep around the edges of stones and other foreign bodies and may eventually create leaks.

It is possible that rock may be encountered during the course of the excavation. A small outcrop could be blasted away but, if it is found in other places, it may be more practicable to raise the sides of the lakes high enough to obtain the desired depth. This difficulty, however, should not arise if a professional survey has been carried out. A rock bottom would not necessarily be leak-proof, as deep fissures may be present. A lining of clay about 20cm thick would prevent such leakage.

Polythene and butyl linings
If the subsoil is found to be altogether pervious and there is no readily available clay, the use of plastic material might be considered but building a fair-sized reservoir with it would be very much more expensive than using natural material because all the excavation work has to be done first, then a sand screed must be laid to prevent sharp stones piercing the liner. After that, a specialist firm is usually required to lay the

plastic material. Finally, a layer of earth and sand is spread over the bottom in order to prevent ultra violet light degrading the liner. Details of construction, including a 'do it yourself' method of joining sheets of liner, will be given in the next chapter.

In the U K, the government department responsible for agriculture, horticulture and fisheries will often give a grant for the construction of a reservoir or lake if it is considered that the cost is justified and it issues booklets containing very helpful advice on the installation of a water supply. Similar facilities are usually offered by governments in most countries and it is advisable to find out if these are available.

If any doubts arise as to the suitability of a site or the quality of the water, it is always wise to contact the Fisheries Officer of the local Water Authority. In the U K, amongst his many administrative duties, he is responsible for providing free technical advice on all matters where fisheries are concerned and directs the activities of a number of fishing bailiffs, each of whom has an allotted area to patrol. The District Civil Engineer will also give free advice if called upon. While Water Authorities often frown on applications to abstract water in most areas where the availability of a natural water supply is limited, they may actively encourage the construction of farm reservoirs and schemes for the storage of water whether for irrigation, crop spraying or for sport, or for a mixture of all three.

2
Lake construction

Provided that the quality of the water is suitable for trout, the supply adequate and the subsoil sufficiently impervious, the next step is to consult a civil engineer with experience in lake building, and ask him to survey the site and draw up a plan for building the type of lake required.

It would be very helpful to the engineer and more economical if, at this stage, much thought is given to the detailed planning of the lake margins. Before the final drawings are completed, an attempt must be made to visualize what shape the lake will be when filled with water. This is not as easy as it would seem, even though the engineer will have pegged out the water levels at intervals. It is easier and less costly to follow the lie of the land where possible, but if the finished lake would then be a rather uninteresting oval shape, something must be done to make it look less artificial. The shoreline should be broken up by excavating one or two small bays, the earth from which could be used to build up adjoining promontories. While this may seem to be an unnecessary expense, it will not only make a great difference to the general appearance of the lake, but will also improve the fishing since, by lengthening the shoreline, the shallower water close to the shore, where trout get most of their food, will be increased.

It is also well worth considering the construction of a specially built fishing promontory, extending 15 or 20m into the lake. This would involve driving in heavy girders and shoring up with railway sleepers or similar well-seasoned wood. The central portion can be filled up with rubble or clay. The advantages to the angler of such a construction are considerable. From one position, there is a very wide area over which to fish, both in deep and shallow water. There is no problem of fishing against the wind because one can usually turn one's back to it. Neither is there need to worry about getting a line caught up in long grass or other vegetation. A boat can also be moored securely away from the prevailing wind. From the trout's point of view, a promontory will always be a favourite spot because, when trout are resting, they usually choose a position under a bank or near a submerged object rather than on the smooth floor of the lake. A promontory would provide the ideal place for trout 'lies'. If it is decided not to build a promontory, then it is advisable to make a provision for some sort of landing stage.

It is a good idea to have one or more islands, which would also increase the feeding area for fish, and at this point it is necessary to decide on their size and position. It is better and cheaper to construct an island by cutting it out from completely undisturbed soil, if possible, thereby helping to reduce any problems of bank erosion and sinkage; but it is usually necessary for the top of the island to be built up with clay and then covered with topsoil in order to obtain the necessary height above water level.

A sufficient depth of water is most important for the well-being of trout in both very hot and very cold weather.

Artificially-made lakes for trout should be made with a deep central channel which slopes gradually towards the outflow system, so that if it becomes necessary to empty the lake, all the water is directed to the outflow, leaving no residual pockets. In the author's lake the upper end of the central channel was 1.8m deep. The channel sloped gradually down over a distance of about 80m to give a depth of about 5m at the outflow. This may seem rather deep but it postpones the need to have the lake dredged out. Furthermore, submerged weed will not usually grow at depths below 2m or so, thus providing a clear area for fishing. Most lakes, except those in peaty soils, will silt up in course of time, so it is better to make them sufficiently deep at the beginning.

Silting can be reduced to a certain extent by making a silt trap on the feeder stream. This is done by widening and deepening part of the stream to reduce the rate of flow, thereby giving the water more time to deposit the silt it is carrying. Such a trap could easily be emptied from time to time by a tractor with a bucket attachment, the silt then being used as top dressing on the land. At the same time, the bed of the stream between the silt trap and the lake should be cleaned to a solid foundation if the owner wishes to make a spawning bed. The depth of excavation required would only need to be about 30cm so that when 15cm of gravel has been added, there is about 15cm of water above it, which is a sufficient depth for spawning trout.

These smaller jobs, though not essential, are very well worth considering before the final plans are made. With the machines on site and before the lake is full, they could be done relatively cheaply and would add considerable value, in the long run, to the lake as a fishing water.

When the owner is satisfied that everything required to be done is included in the final drawings, these can be made up and, in the U K, are sent off to the area Water Authority in order for planning permission to be obtained. Note, however, that all details concerning the construction, width, length and depth of the lake, and the use to which the water will be put, must be shown in the drawings; permissions or agreements with other bodies or with neighbouring landowners must be included.

If a lake is to be used for irrigation purposes, for which a grant may be given in the U K, a copy of the plans must also be sent to the local office of the Ministry of Agriculture and Fisheries which will require to know the total capacity of the proposed lake, together with the details of the water supply and outlet. Such regulations and requirements will obviously differ quite widely from one country to another and from one state to another, some rules being stricter than others, depending on many factors such as population density, annual rainfall and geographical variations, but it is always advisable for a would-be lake builder to become well acquainted with such rules.

If the plans are approved, in the U K they must be published in a local paper and in the London Gazette. They must also be made available for inspection by the public for one month. If no objections are raised the work can proceed, the first step being to seek tenders from contractors who are experienced in this kind of work. In some cases the owner may have his own machine and his own labour and he could therefore do most of the work himself at less cost provided, of course, he enlists the supervisory services of a civil engineer.

Outflow systems
Whenever water is impounded by means of a dam, an efficient outflow system is required and one which is capable of dealing with a sudden rise in water level. Under no circumstances whatever should water be allowed to flow over the top of a dam, a happening which might give rise to dangerous flooding and very heavy costs for damages suffered by others. A civil engineer will give advice on the most suitable type of outflow system, taking into account the volume of water to be impounded, the catchment area of the supply stream and the liability of

24

flooding in the locality.

Some of the Water Authority's more important requirements in the UK are given below and it is advisable to check that they have been included in the plans:

1. Freeboard required is 1m above water level or normal spillway level. Emergency pipe level must be 30cm above normal water level.
2. The minimum top width of the dam must be 2.5m and the upstream slope shall not be steeper than 1 vertical to 2.5 horizontal.
3. The downstream slope of the dam will depend on the maximum height of the dam and must be in accordance with the following table.

Downstream slope not steeper than	Maximum permissible height of dam
1 in 2	3.9m
1 in 2.5	5.4m
1 in 3	8.1m

4. The plan must provide for adequate excavation along the whole length of the base of the dam to prevent water passing under it (*Figs 8a* and *8b*).
5. The subsoil used for dam construction must contain sufficient clay and must be laid down in layers not exceeding 22cm.
6. It is necessary to sow grass seed on and around the dam on completion. Grasses should be of a low maintenance variety because of restricted access for cutting. Perennial ryegrass is too vigorous. Creeping red fescue, chewing fescue, smooth-stalked meadow grass and browntop should be used. These are all slow growing and provide a dense cover with thick root formation to bind the topsoil. No trees may be planted on it. The volume of water to be impounded and the volume of soil excavated must be stated.
7. Reservoirs in the UK with a capacity of 5 million gallons (20 megalitres) or over will need a special permit submitted by a civil engineer appointed by the Secretary of State. In the USA a similar permit is required from the Department of Water Resources and the Department of Environmental Conservation for water capacities over 500,000 cubic feet.
8. Provision for drainage is usually necessary while the work is in progress and in certain cases allowance for a residual overflow must be made while the lake is filling in order not to stop the water supply downstream which may be required for livestock.

9. If it is proposed to construct the dam of concrete, bricks or other materials, sufficiently detailed drawings must be submitted in order that the safety of the structure can be confirmed.

There are three main types of outflow system which are used for small and medium sized lakes. They are:

1. The funnel system or vertical overflow pipe system
2. The spillway
3. The monk

The basic principles of each one will be described, with a more detailed account of the work of building the funnel system and the construction of the dam. Such measurements as are given are merely to indicate approximate size and are not specific. Engineers' plans are not always easy to follow and the purpose of a fairly detailed description is to help any would-be lake builder to understand more exactly what is being done from day to day. Moreover, if the contractor is aware that the owner knows how the job ought to be done, then there is less likelihood of slipshod workmanship.

The funnel system
This type of installation is generally used for medium to large sized lakes where there is big catchment area and above average rainfall. This was the system used by the author when constructing a lake in Shropshire, U K (*frontispiece*), which had a capacity of about 17,000m³ (approximately 3.75 million gallons) and an area of about 2.2 acres (0.9ha).

The principle of this system is shown in *Fig 7(a)*. The excess of water spills over the top of the funnel E and falls into the chamber O, from where it flows through the pipe B under the dam and out. One advantage of this type of outflow method is that it can be placed well out from the shore and away from any outside interference. The entry to the funnel is covered by a wire cage to prevent fish from escaping and to stop debris from getting in. The funnel is sufficiently wide to allow a man to inspect the chamber O by climbing down the rungs embedded in the concrete.

The first job was to make certain that the site remained dry while the work was in progress. This presented no difficulty as it had been a dry summer and the feeder streams were very low. By using a petrol-driven

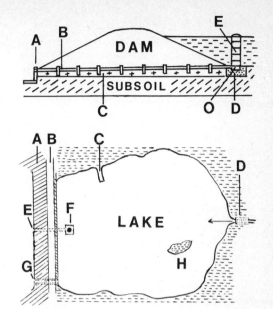

Fig 7a The funnel system
A – head-wall and spill-slab
B – concrete outflow pipe with con-
    crete supports
C – base of dam
D – concrete base
E – vertical funnel
O – chamber

Fig 7b Funnel system viewed
    from above in relation to lake
A – outer slope of dam
B – driveway across dam
C – artificial promontory
D – supply stream with spawning
    cage
E – outflow pipe
F – funnel system
G – emergency overflow pipe
H – island

pump with piping, the water was easily cleared from the site and no diversion channel was needed. The contractor then cleared the topsoil from the whole site and this was piled up in a convenient place as near as possible to where the future dam was to be constructed, because the soil had to be used eventually to cover the completed dam. Excavation of the subsoil to form the base of the dam was then started.

The base was dug well down to at least 1m below what was to be the level of the lake floor (*Fig 8a*). This keying-in of the base into the subsoil is very important and prevents water from tracking underneath the dam. If there is any doubt about there being sufficient clay content in the subsoil, it is advisable to take further precautions by digging three trenches about 1m deep (*Fig 8b*) and then backfill them with soil of high clay content.

Having dug out the base to the required depth, the contractor began backfilling with clay up to a level where he could start laying the outflow pipe B (*Fig 7a*). Concrete supports, measuring 60cm × 60cm and 90cm deep, were built and so spaced that the joints of the outflow pipe B would rest on them. The concrete pipes, each 3.6m long and 30cm diameter were then manoeuvred into position on to the concrete supports and the joints sealed with cement and an outer covering of

27

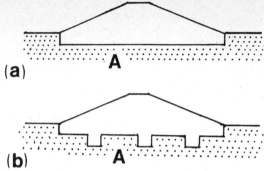

Fig 8a and b   Keying in the base of
  a dam
A – subsoil

(a)

(b)

bitumen. The inclusion of rubber rings at the joints gives slight flexibility to the pipe and may prevent a leak if sinkage occurs.

Each joint was then fixed to its support by a capping of concrete. The gradient from the lake end of the pipe to the discharging end, a distance of 30m, was about 60cm. The concrete collars, apart from supporting the outflow pipe, serve also to prevent the seepage of water along the outside of the pipe by acting as 'spurs' which interrupt any small leakage channel which may find its way along the pipe.

While the concrete was setting, excavation to build a concrete foundation for the vertical funnel was begun. Because of the weight and height of the funnel, the base had to be very solid, about 3m square × 90cm deep. *Figure 9* shows the lake end of the concrete pipe B incorporated into the foundation, on the top of which a chamber O has been made; into this chamber a short metal drainage pipe D, 23cm diameter with a screw cap, was built in.

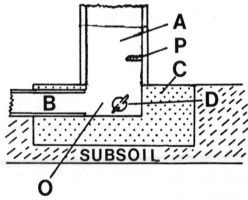

Fig 9   Section through the base of
  the funnel
A – lowest concrete ring (cutaway)
P – foot rung
C – concrete base
D – cap on drain
O – chamber
B – outflow pipe

28

The next step was to start carefully covering up the outflow pipe, the concrete collars of which must be quite dry. At first this was a manual job, clay having to be pounded tightly in and around the pipes. When the pipes had been well covered, the earth-moving machine pushed the clay carefully up to the pipes for further manual spreading. A machine worked each side of the pipe gradually building up the clay around it in layers, each about 10–15cm deep. The danger of cracking or displacing the pipe by the great weight of the machine had to be guarded against and it was not until about 1m of clay had been laid over the pipe, that the machine could cross it very slowly, without risk of damage.

Proof that the pipe was not damaged in any way was later confirmed by the contractor himself, who was drawn through the pipe lying on his back on a specially constructed trolley with a rope at each end – a most unpleasant form of inspection to say the least, and one requiring considerable courage, the pipe being barely wide enough to admit a fully-grown man. Work on the dam continued with putting down layer upon layer of clay each about 15cm deep until the overall height was about 6.5m, allowing 60cm for sinkage. The width of the top of the dam was sufficient for two vehicles to pass one another and the finished surface was slightly cambered from front to back to allow water to run off it. The gradient of each slope was 1 in 3.

A head-wall A and concrete slab C were then built at the mouth of the outflow pipe (*Fig 10*). The head-wall is important and gives stability to the end of the outflow pipe. The sloped concrete slab prevents gradual erosion of the base of the dam by water discharging from the outflow pipe.

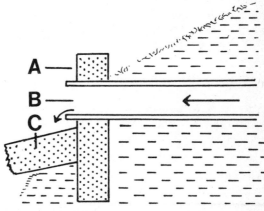

Fig 10 Head-wall
A – head-wall
B – mouth of outflow pipe
C – concrete slab

As soon as the concrete foundation of the funnel system was dry, the contractor started to lift the heavy concrete rings into position. Each ring had a diameter of 90cm and a height of 1m. Five rings were used, each being carefully fitted together and the joints sealed with cement, then covered with bitumen. The top of the completed drainage funnel was now about 1.5m below the top of the dam, giving the required freeboard after allowing for sinkage of the dam. When the concrete was dry, it was then possible to climb down inside the funnel on the rungs fixed in the concrete and unscrew the cap D on the drainage pipe (*Fig 9*). Any water on the site then flowed through this drain and no further pumping was necessary.

While the funnel was being built, the earth-moving machines were excavating the remainder of the site to a depth sufficient to make the central channel at the upper end of the lake about 1.8m deep when the lake was full. The channel was made to slope gradually down towards the funnel system, where the depth was to be about 5m, as mentioned previously.

An island about 10m long and 5m wide was next cut out of undisturbed soil, but the lie of land was such that a lot of clay had to be added on top to raise it about 2m above water level, allowing for sinkage. Topsoil was spread over the island which was later sown with grass seed.

The lake had three small feeder streams and two of these were made wider and deeper to form spawning beds.

Another task was to make a landing stage with old railway sleepers, and around this the bottom of the lake was deepened, making a convenient place for releasing trout after their journey from the fish farm, and for mooring a boat. It was not possible to construct a fishing promontory for economic reasons.

Emergency overflow pipes

For both funnel and spillway systems (*Figs 7a* and *17*) it is compulsory in the U K to put into the dam two emergency overflow pipes of about 45cm diameter and 30cm above the level of the lake water. It is more convenient if they are dug in after the dam is completed and there is then less risk of damage to the pipes from heavy machines passing over them. If a spillway is used, they are put in at the end of the dam opposite to the spillway. If the funnel system is employed, the pipes can be put in at either end. *Figure 11* shows the emergency pipes on the lake side of the dam and *Fig 12* shows their position on the outer slope. A channel C must be dug in such a direction that any overflow from the emergency pipes B will be directed well away from the base of the dam to J (*Fig 12*) where it would join the main outflow from under the dam if the funnel

Fig 11   Emergency overflow pipes on lake side edge of the dam which is on the right

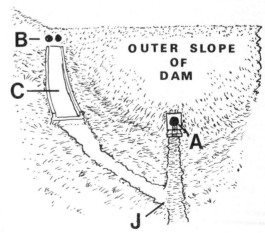

Fig 12   Outflow channel for emergency overflow pipes
A – outflow pipe from lake
B – emergency overflow pipes
C – concrete channel
J – junction of channel with outflow from lake

system is used. If a spillway is used, it would join the original bed of the stream.

After the emergency overflow pipes had been installed, the dam was covered with top soil and seeded with the type of grass seed already mentioned. Apart from tidying up, the work was finished. It was started at the beginning of June 1975, and completed on August 5 of the same year; the weather was favourable and the contractor proved most efficient. The Water Authority gave permission for filling to start, so someone climbed down the funnel (*Fig 9*) and replaced the screw cap D, thus shutting off the drainage system and causing the lake to start filling slowly. A strong wire fish screen (*Fig 16*) was fixed to the top of the funnel in such a way that it could be easily removed for inside inspection. On December 25 of the same year the lake was full and water began to flow down the funnel.

Leakage in a dam

In normal conditions it is unlikely that any leakage will occur outwards from the pipe system, because the water flowing through the pipes is not under pressure and its movement is due to gravity only. If leaks do

Fig 13   The top of the author's dam

occur, they will be 'into' rather than 'out of' the system. For example, if there is an imperfect seal between two of the concrete rings in the funnel, water will force its way through, with a pressure directly proportioned to the depth of the leak below water level.

The most likely point for a leak to occur is into the outflow pipe between the base of the funnel and the base of the dam, where the pipe has the least covering of clay. If a leak starts here, it will tend to get larger with the pressure of water and may lower the water level of the lake to such an extent that water no longer goes down the funnel.

If such a leak should occur and it is only small, it can often be successfully sealed off by using an aluminium complex silicate mixed

Fig 14   A dam with insufficient freeboard and not sown with grass. Erosion is starting

with ground-up ashes which, when in contact with water, has the property of swelling up to many times its normal size; if several bags of this are emptied over the area where a leak is suspected, it will be carried in by the water current to the leakage point and will hopefully seal it off. Another similar substance called Bentonite can also be used. It is a form of clay, mined in Dakota and sold as grey powder in 50kg bags. It is spread into the water at the rate of about 10kg per square metre over the suspected place of leakage.

The funnel itself can easily be inspected for leaks by looking over the top from a boat and, if there happens to be a leak, it would be clearly visible and could be efficiently sealed off by a diver plugging it from outside.

A check must be made for a leak if damp patches are found anywhere

Fig 15   A reservoir with a good, wide bank but insufficient freeboard

on the outer slope of the dam; a leak under pressure always becomes larger. The contractor must be informed immediately and he will probably take action according to the procedure outlined above. If he is unsuccessful, however, the water level of the lake must be lowered until the leak stops and the contractor will then have to find some way of reinforcing the dam. Damp patches in the first year or two after construction do not necessarily spell danger and are often due to 'sweating out' of the clay, but such patches should be carefully monitored for any change in the amount of moisture.

The real danger of a dam bursting arises if, for some reason, the water begins to flow over the top. A small channel is eroded into the topsoil; at first it enlarges slowly and looks fairly harmless but the deeper it becomes, the more the water pressure from the lake builds up. The channel continues to widen and deepen at an alarming rate until a section of the dam is washed away.

Even a very well-constructed dam should be inspected at regular intervals. Moles (*Talpa Europaea*) can cause a lot of trouble if their burrows extend below water level; their breeding burrows are often about a metre deep. A watch must be kept for other burrowing animals such as rabbits or foxes. If the grass on the dam is kept short, either by

Fig 16 The mouth of the funnel with fish guard

35

cutting or by grazing a few sheep, inspection will be made much easier.

One of the chief advantages of the funnel system was that very little debris collected round the mouth of the funnel, almost all of it being moved to the shoreline by wind and wave action and only once, in three years, was it necessary to move some branches.

Earth-moving machines

The best type of machine to use for dam construction is one which scrapes the soil away layer by layer rather than one which digs it out in large lumps, as with a bucket type digger. A soil with a high clay content thus gets more finely divided and when this is spread onto the dam, the constant to and fro movement of the earth moving machine compacts it down firmly. Moreover, any large piece of flint or rock can be more easily seen and removed.

Perhaps the most efficient machine for making small lakes and ponds (or 'dugouts' as they are often called in the U S A) is the bulldozer (*Fig 23*) which has a 2m wide curved blade mounted on a tracklaying tractor. It is an excellent machine for finishing off a bank and tidying up, which bigger machines cannot do so well. It cannot be used in very wet conditions. For larger excavations, the so-called 'dragline' can be used. This consists of a crane mounted on a tracklaying tractor from which the driver manipulates a large metal scoop. This machine has an all-round reach of 15m and, when the subsoil is under water, is particularly useful because it can operate from dry land, digging away each side and depositing the soil on the banks. For digging trenches or test holes a tractor with hydraulically operated buckets specially designed for digging is used.

The spillway

This system can be used in small to medium-sized lakes in conjunction with a dam. It is more suitable for sites where the supply stream is fairly steady and not subject to sudden variations as often happens in very hilly districts. The principle is that water overflowing from the lake is guided down a concrete channel at the side of the dam, to join the original course of the stream at D (*Fig 17*).

A dam for the spillway system is constructed in a similar fashion as for the funnel system. Some provision may have to be made to keep the site dry while a concrete pipe, which will afterwards act as a drain for the lake, is being laid. The diameter of this pipe will depend on the

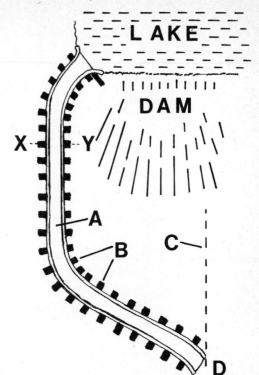

Fig 17 Diagram of a spillway in
relation to a dam

A – spillway
B – concrete supports
C – course of original stream
D – end of spillway
XY – see *Fig 19*

volume of water in the lake and the rate of inflow into it will be
calculated by the civil engineer. When the concrete pipe is completed,
water may be allowed to flow through it, while work on the dam continues. When the dam has reached the required height, the construction
of the concrete spillway can be started, the detailed structure and size of
which will also have been planned by the civil engineer, taking into
account the maximum amount of water likely to pass over it under
severe storm conditions. The structure is in itself very simple, but the
important part is to construct the concrete supports B of the channel in
such a way that there is no danger of sinkage. Any movement of the
concrete supports may cause cracking of the spillway channel A, giving
rise to leakage and progressive undermining of the channel (*Fig 18*). The
number of supports necessary depends on the gradient and the type of
subsoil but the distance between supports should never be more than
3m. If the soil has been disturbed, the distance between supports should

Fig 18   Collapsed end of spillway due to weak foundations

be less. The channel should always be constructed with the least possible gradient. *Figure 19* represents a cross section of the spillway resting on a support (XY in *Fig 17*). It will be seen that concrete spurs SS' have been built above the level of the water in the spillway. This is an important point, the purpose of which is to counteract the natural tendency of water to creep between concrete and the surrounding soil.

The point at which a leak is most likely to occur is at E (*Fig 20*) where the inside lip of the spillway lies adjacent to the dam. If a leak starts there, it will become gradually larger until a serious leak and damage occurs. To counteract this, the inner wall of the spillway B and the first

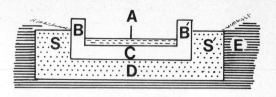

Fig 19 Section through spillway
and foundations, XY of *Fig 17*
A   – water level in spillway
BB' – side walls
C   – floor of spillway
D   – concrete support
SS' – spurs of concrete support
E   – dam

concrete support C should each be prolonged about 2m towards the dam. Clay must be packed down round both.

Provision must be made for a fish screen D (*Fig 20*) and this should be so positioned that a person can walk on the spillway in order to remove debris. Several strong steel posts, to which a fish screen can be attached, must be embedded in the concrete before it has dried out. Provision must also be made for padlocking the screen to the posts.

Another important point is that the course of the spillway must be planned in such a way that it is well away from the base of the dam, joining the course of the original stream at D (*Fig 17*). If a leak from the spillway should occur, it is then unlikely to cause any undermining of the dam.

In the U K, permission must be obtained to starting filling a lake and a civil engineer is required to carry out an inspection of the site. If permission is given, the lake-side end of the drain pipe is sealed off with a rubber cap or similar device and the lake will start to fill. It is important to fix a long-handled metal rod across the cap to act as a marker before

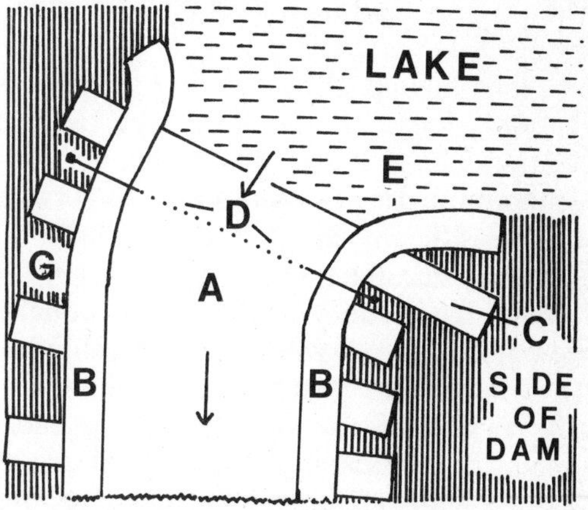

Fig 20 Mouth of spillway
A – floor of spillway
B – inner wall of spillway prolonged
C – first concrete support prolonged
D – fish screen
E – potentially weak spot
G – bank

Fig 21   A spillway partly blocked by a tree trunk and rocks

the lake fills up. Provided that the marker remains in position it will be easier to locate the cap if the lake has to be drained, but even then it will be buried in mud and its removal against water pressure will not be easy without the use of some form of underwater diving equipment.

The difficulty in emptying the lake, when silting-up has occurred, is the chief disadvantage of the spillway. It is better used where the supply stream has a rocky bed or flows through chalk, where silt, carried down in times of flood, will be considerably less. In the U S A the spillway is invariably used for the many small lakes and ponds which are built by the owners of country homes and cabins as a water supply, and for fishing and bathing. Instead of draining by a pipe under the dam with all its problems of silting, it is sometimes preferable to pump or syphon the

Fig 22 Some of six small lakes made in a valley by one man and one machine. A spillway can be seen on the right of the first two dams

Fig 23 The machine that made the previous lakes

water out, which is easy enough until the water becomes thick with sediment. The U S A Department of Agriculture is trying to design a new type of hose-syphon especially to cope with draining out silt. This would certainly solve many problems as well as reduce expense. Otherwise the spillway system is very satisfactory but it should be regularly inspected to clear debris from the fish screen, which, if it becomes badly blocked, may cause water to flow over the side walls around the concrete supports.

The monk system
This system is used extensively in Europe, Asia, the Far East and Africa for the cultivation of edible fish such as carp, catfish, tilapia and others, all of which thrive better in warm waters. The size of the ponds in which the fish are kept varies greatly between 0.25ha and 3 or 4ha or more, the depth never being more than 1 or 2m deep. The word 'pond' as opposed to 'lake', is defined as a small body of fresh water in which the littoral zone is relatively large and the limnetic and profundal zones are small or absent. In simpler terms, the water is shallow for a good distance from the shore and there may or may not be deeper water in the middle. In the U S A, a body of water perhaps only 40m across and 3m deep in the middle, often with very little shallow water, is called a 'farm pond' or 'dugout'. The author's two acre lake in Shropshire, U K, was also invariably called a 'pond' by the local inhabitants. The word is therefore somewhat confusing and its meaning must be taken in context.

Ponds for fish cultivation are usually placed in series, each having its own monk system with the water flowing from one pond to another. The risk of flooding is small because the main source of water is controlled by a sluice. Regular emptying and cleaning out, which is necessary for intensive fish cultivation, present no difficulties because diversion channels are usually installed round the ponds. The monk system could very well be used for an ornamental pond in a district where there is no danger of sudden flooding and where the water supply can be controlled.

Provided the sub-soil has a sufficient clay content, the pond is excavated from the centre and the soil is packed into banks round the margins of the pond. Each bank must be carefully constructed as if building a miniature dam all round the pond, the foundations having been dug down to a solid base. A central, sloping channel, as described for the funnel system, is then made, directed towards where the monk will be built, giving a depth at the monk of about 2m. All the banks or dikes should be at least 1m wide on top, and planted with grass or turfed.

Another confusing word is the term 'dike'. In some European countries a bank is called a 'dike', meaning an embankment to hold back water. A 'dike' can also mean a ditch or artificial channel and, perhaps even more perplexing, in Scotland it can mean a dry stone wall.

Construction

The monk, though sometimes constructed in wood, is usually made with two concrete side walls, and a back wall, each about 15cm thick, standing on a solid concrete foundation (*Fig 24*). The top of the monk should not be more than about 30cm above the level of the top of the bank. If it is made too high, it becomes difficult to slide out the sluice boards C. On the inner surface of each side wall there are three slots which are continued across the base. Into the two slots A (*Figs 24* and *25*) in the middle of the monk, are fitted sluice boards of seasoned oak, one on top of the other, and the intervening space is well packed with moist clay B.

If this is done properly, only very minor leakage, of no consequence, can occur. On each sluice board C there is a strong metal ring by means of which the boards can be hooked up if it is necessary to lower the water level. The third slot at the mouth of the monk is for the fish screen

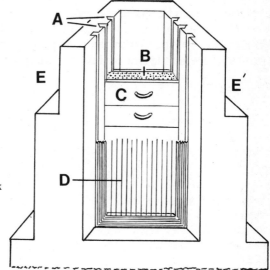

Fig 24 Front view of the monk
system

A – slots for sluice boards
B – clay packing
C – sluice board with metal ring
D – fish screen
EE′ – shoulders of monk

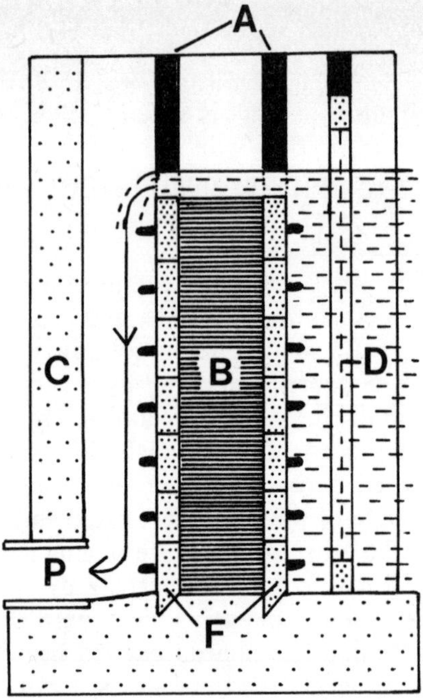

Fig 25 Side view of monk
A – slots for sluice boards
B – clay packing
C – back wall
D – fish screen
F – bottom sluice boards
P – outflow pipe

D, the top of which must be well above the water level to prevent fish from escaping. The shape and size of the slots are important. If the slots were rectangular it might be very difficult to remove a board if the wood became swollen, but when the rear part of the slot is sloped as shown (*Fig 26*) there is little risk of this happening.

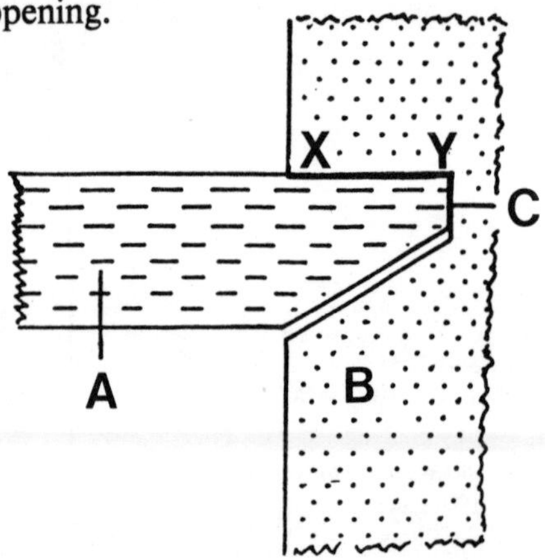

Fig 26 Detail of slot for sluice
  boards
A   – sluice board
B   – side wall
C   – slot
XY – pressure surface

44

Another important point is that the depth of the slot should be about 6cm. The sluice boards are forced by the pressure of the water against the surface XY which must be well smoothed off in order to secure a good seal against leakage. Slots should be finished off with a mixture of 1 in 2 cement and sand to get a smooth finish. Alternatively, a metal lining can be used for the slots, but rust may eventually cause difficulty in sliding the sluice boards up and down.

The outflow pipe should be about 30cm in diameter and made of precast concrete laid in the fashion described for the funnel system. The floor of the monk behind the outflow pipe must be slightly sloped (*Fig 25*). The emerging outflow pipe must be extended well clear of the bank so that the flow of water either spills directly into another pond or flows out through a head-wall on to a concrete slab (*Fig 10*).

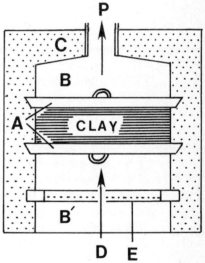

Fig 27   Monk viewed from above
A   – top sluice board
BB′ – floor of monk
C   – back wall
D   – direction of flow
E   – fish screen
P   – outflow pipe

Monks may be sited 1 or 2m out from the bank to make it more difficult for vandals or poachers to meddle with them. In such a case, to get to the monk it is necessary to have a movable walk-way or strong plank from the top of the bank on to the monk, where it is fixed into hooks. The person manipulating the sluice boards or clearing the fish screen can stand on the 'shoulders' of the monk (*Figs 24* and *28*). It is necessary also to have a hinged iron grating A (*Fig 28*), or something similar, which can be locked down over the top of the monk to prevent unwarranted interference with the sluice boards.

45

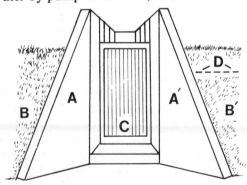

Fig 28 Oblique view of top of
   monk built away from the bank
A – hinged grating with lock
B – movable walkway
E – shoulder of monk

A monk can also be sited close in to the bank, in which case it is advisable to build out concrete wings AA' (*Fig 29*) on each side of the entrance. If this is done, there will be far less likelihood of a leak starting alongside the outflow pipe under the bank, because clay can be packed hard behind each concrete wing.

Sometimes a catching chamber is built at the opening of the outflow pipe. The purpose of this is to eliminate unwanted coarse fish or pike which have found their way in. When the pond is drained, the sluice boards are hooked up one by one and the fish screen taken away. Most of the fish will come through the outflow pipe and into the catchment chamber when the pond is nearly empty; they will be accompanied by much mud, which makes sorting difficult. This can be counteracted by bringing in a supply of clear water by pump or channel, in order to clear

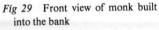

Fig 29 Front view of monk built
   into the bank
AA' – concrete wings
BB' – banks
C – fish screen
D – water level

the mud away. In coarse fish farms, the chamber is divided into sections by screens of varying gauges, so that the fish tend to grade themselves automatically according to size.

Fish screens

Any well-stocked fishery must have some means of preventing the escape of fish. Rainbow trout are great escapers and in fish farms are often seen trying to jump up into the outflow pipes between ponds, in an attempt to get into the water above. The author has seen one swimming up a spillway in spite of a very strong current of water. Brown trout, provided that they are not overcrowded and conditions are to their liking, seem to have much less urge to escape and if they can find a good 'lie', will remain there and defend their territory vigorously. In the spawning season they try to move upstream, looking for suitable spawning beds, but after the eggs are laid will probably return to their former territory.

Fish screens must always be made strong enough to hold up against the worst conditions. If a screen gets blocked with weed and there is an accompanying flood, the pressure against the screen may be sufficient to displace it, unless it is strongly constructed. This applies particularly to the spillway system where leaves, weed and branches may become jammed against the screen by a strong current.

Fish screens are sometimes made with a series of vertical iron bars about 2cm apart or from strong galvanized wire of about 3cm square mesh. For fingerling trout (10–15cm length) a smaller meshed wire screen would be needed. It is always a problem to find a screen which allows the maximum of debris to pass through it without the fish escaping. Long strands of weed are the chief cause of obstruction and it is a tedious and cold job removing them by hand. This difficulty can be greatly reduced by using a double screen, one fixed and the other movable. The fixed screen can be made of strong, square-meshed galvanized wire about 3mm thick and can be obtained in all gauges. The size of fish put into the lake will determine the size of gauge to be chosen but, obviously, the bigger the gauge, the less chance of debris collecting.

The movable screen (*Fig 30*) is made of a smaller gauge wire than that of the fixed screen. Its lower part is bent at a right angle to form a shelf upon which all the debris falls when it is pulled up. This type of screen would be for use on the front of a monk from which it can be suspended, the force of the current pressing it against the walls of the monk. For the

47

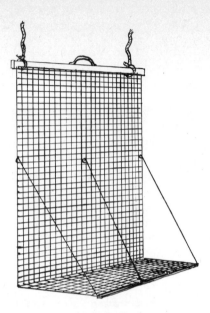

Fig 30   Movable wire debris screen

spillway, wider but shorter screens, made in a similar way, will be required. They are very easy to make and to handle and any debris caught up can be tipped on to the bank and the screens replaced in the space of a few minutes (*Fig 31*).

If any weed has got through to the fixed screen, it can usually be removed by using a stiff brush. The importance of placing the fixed screen in an easily accessible position for regular cleaning has been stated already, but cannot be over-emphasized.

Standing on a spillway to clean the fish screen can be quite hazardous because its surface becomes covered with slime and the pressure of water around the feet makes it difficult to keep a firm foothold. It is therefore advisable to fix some form of hand-rail such as a length of old iron pipe, immediately above and parallel to the fish screen. Such a simple device can save someone from a painful and undignified fall.

Plastic linings

As previously mentioned, plastic linings are more suitable for reservoirs than for fishing lakes for the following reasons.

It is not possible to have a fringe of vegetation such as sedge along the shoreline because the edge of the liner covers the ground on which such plants would normally grow. Without such vegetation, the usual insect

Fig 31 Emptying a movable screen

life of a lake could not develop and perhaps, more important, anglers would be exposed to the full view of any trout within a distance of 20m or so. Aquatic plants, either submerged or semi-submerged, would only have sand in which to take root unless soil is added after the liner is laid down and this would be difficult to do without damage to the liner and much expense.

The wear and tear of anglers' boots on the edges of the liner may lead to splits developing. This could be counteracted to some extent by having fixed fishing stations where coconut or other form of matting could be laid.

Finally, in the author's experience, field mice and burrowing animals can give a great deal of trouble if they can work their way under the edge of the liner where they find a dry, well protected nesting site and will, for one reason or another, start gnawing holes in the plastic liner. This produces a slow leak which is almost impossible to locate.

It is said that butyl liners will last for 50 years. Perhaps this would be so if a reservoir lined with butyl was used strictly for water storage but if used for a fishery as well, apart from the day to day wear and tear on the edges, an angler might fall into the water in the excitement of landing a fish and in his struggles to get up the steep slope of the sides, he might do severe damage to the liner below the surface.

Construction of lined reservoirs
These are usually sited on a flat area of ground where there is a convenient natural water supply *eg* from a small stream or by abstraction of water from a main stream by gravity or pump (*Fig 5*). For reasons of economy and ease of working they are usually made rectangular in shape unless required for ornamental purposes.

Starting from the centre of the site, the soil is pushed to the sides to build up banks of equal height all round, the internal gradient of the banks being about 1 in 3. The bottom of the reservoir should be flat, making it much easier to lay the liner. At this stage, provision must be made for an outflow pipe for whichever of the three systems is to be used and, if the site becomes waterlogged, pumping equipment will be needed to remove the water.

When the excavation work has been completed, the surfaces of the sides and bottom must be smoothed off and inspected for any sharp projections which might pierce the lining. As a further precaution, it is advisable to put down a layer of sand on the bottom, 4 or 5cm deep, as a protective bedding for the liner. It would be of no use to put sand on the sloping sides as it would gradually slip towards the middle. The sides are therefore covered later with a layer of polyester protective matting. This is a soft but durable material about 2mm thick made up of compressed polyester fibres. The weight recommended for use is 300mgm per square metre and is usually supplied with the liner (*Fig 32*). If there is any likelihood of weeds emerging anywhere under the liner, sodium chlorate should be applied, but this is unlikely if a fair depth of topsoil has been removed.

When all the work of excavation has been finished, the construction of

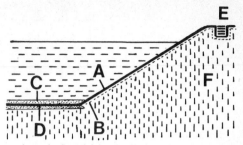

Fig 32 Cross section of the edge of
a lined reservoir
A – liner
B – polyester protective matting
C – top layer of sand
D – under layer of sand
E – trench to hold down liner
F – bank

an outflow system must be started and should be built on the same lines
as previously described in this chapter. When this has been completed,
the reservoir is ready for the liner to be laid down. It is advisable, if
expense allows, to call in a specialist firm to do the work but in some
countries such contractors may not be available and an alternative
method of joining sheets of liner will be described which does not involve
heat welding. The liner arrives in rolls varying in width from 5 to 10m
and the price naturally varies according to thickness and durability.
Starting at one end, the liner is spread out across the floor and sides of
the reservoir, each piece being heat-welded to the adjoining piece, a job
requiring considerable skill. The edges of the sheeting are fixed into a
trench dug all around the top of the banks (*Fig 32*). The trench E should
measure 30cm wide and 30cm deep and be dug about 0.5m away from
the edge of the slope. When the liner, with the polyester protective
matting under it, is in place, the trench is back-filled with soil which will
hold the liner firmly in position. To prevent damage to the liner by sharp
objects while the work is in progress on the floor of the reservoir, it is
advisable to put down a layer of sand over the liner as soon as it has
been welded.

When the lining of the reservoir is complete, the sheeting round the
concrete structures and pipes must be sealed. This is done on straight
surfaces by cutting a 6 × 4cm chase into the concrete into which the edge
of the sheeting is inserted (*Fig 33*). A wooden batten, 5 × 2.5cm is then
placed on top of the sheeting and pinned down into the concrete. Epoxy
resin should then be applied to fill in all gaps and to cover the batten.
Special pipe collars are factory made and already welded to the sheeting.
The collars are fitted round pipes where necessary and fastened with
adhesive tape and jubilee clips.

Instead of vulcanization, an alternative method of joining together
two sheets of liner is described in *Trout Farming Manual* (Stevenson). A

51

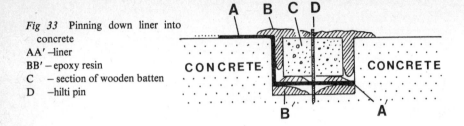

Fig 33 Pinning down liner into
concrete
AA' –liner
BB' – epoxy resin
C – section of wooden batten
D –hilti pin

trench about 25cm × 25cm is dug out along the line where two sheets
are to be joined. The edges of each sheet are aligned together and put
into the trench (*Fig 34*, A). The trench is filled with heavy earth or clay
and compacted down B. The upper sheet is then drawn across in the
direction of the arrow C to lie flat alongside the other as in D. The junction so formed, if carefully done, should be reasonably watertight.
Before filling starts it is often necessary to obtain permission from the
local Water Authority. In the U K it is always necessary but in some
countries it may not be required, much depending on the volume of
water impounded.

Ornamental lakes, with a much more attractive appearance, are made
in exactly the same way but would be relatively much more expensive
because much of the sheeting has to be cut away and wasted in order to
give the lake an irregular shape.

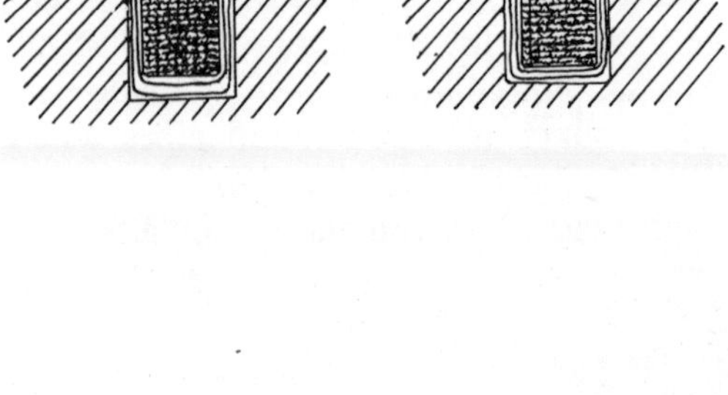

Fig 34 Alternative method of joining liner

3
Stocking and letting

When a lake has been newly constructed and filled, there should be no hurry to stock it with fish. In about a month the water will clear but the natural ecology may take a year to develop.

Before introducing fish of any kind into a fishery in the U K, whether river or lake, permission must be obtained from the local fishery authority who will need to know the number and type of fish to be stocked, the time and date of stocking and the name of the supplier. These precautions are very necessary to prevent the spread of disease. The fishery authority is in a position to know whether there has been any disease in its area and if any fish farm is a suspect source. If permission to stock is granted, the lake owner can be reasonably certain that healthy fish will be acquired. In all countries where there is intensive cultivation of fish, similar regulations would exist with which the lake owner must conform before stocking.

The best time to start introducing fish is at the end of April or the beginning of May when winged insect life is more plentiful, though aquatic creatures, the trout's main source of food, would still be somewhat scarce, so supplementary feeding would be necessary for a time. The problem for the owner is to know how many fish to put in and the answer depends, long-term, on the food supply in the lake and not necessarily on its size. A large lake with a rocky bottom and poor weed growth would be able to support fewer fish than a smaller lake with a silt bottom having plenty of weed teeming with aquatic creatures. An extreme example is the fish farm, where thousands of fish grow rapidly in a very small volume of water because there is an abundance of artificial food.

No two lakes are exactly alike in their capacity to supply food; it is therefore better to err on the side of too few fish rather than too many.

The stocking of a newly-made lake in which the natural food supply is not yet fully established, should be at the rate of about 100 trout per acre (0.4ha). If they grow well in the first year, more can be added in the following year but if too many are put in at the start, the owner may well be left with many undersized fish and this is unsatisfactory both for the angler and the owner who may need to have the stock reduced by netting out.

The choice of trout to be stocked lies mainly between brown and rainbow trout which are most suited to a temperate climate and, being more commonly bred in fish farms, are more readily available.

The brown trout (*Salmo trutta*) is indigenous to northern and western Europe, North Africa and northwestern Asia and there are several subspecies in the Mediterranean and Black Sea areas. It has been introduced to many countries where the environmental conditions are suitable and it can now be found in North and South America, parts of Africa, Australia, New Zealand and Kashmir.

The rainbow trout (*Salmo gairdnerii*) is indigenous to certain tributaries of the Sacramento River in North America. It was first introduced to Europe in 1882. It is similar in appearance to the brown trout but it has a red coloration down each side of its body from which it takes its name. It grows faster than a brown trout and can tolerate higher water temperatures. Unlike the brown trout, it has not been known to breed naturally in the U K, except in a few isolated rivers.

The American brook trout (*Salvelinus fontinalis*) must be mentioned also. It was introduced to European waters at the end of the nineteenth century where it has established itself in cool, spring-fed mountain streams but has not been successful as a lake fish in U K. It cross-breeds with both rainbow and brown trout, the hybrids being termed 'cheetahs' and 'tigers', but neither are fertile. The 'brookie' is much favoured in North America as a trout to stock the small, but deep, home ponds. It breeds well and can survive the long winter under ice provided certain precautions are taken.

For a trout fishery to be profitable when open to the public, where the angler wants live sport and a reasonable catch to take home, rainbow trout would seem to be the best fish to choose. When newly introduced from the fish farm they are not difficult to catch and are usually tamer than brown trout. Those that are not immediately caught grow more rapidly than brown trout but they do not live quite as long. This is not of great importance because the aim of a sport fishery is to maintain a rapid turnover of healthy young fish. The flesh of either species depends largely on the food they have been eating. In water where there is ample supply of shrimps, snails and very small crustaceans, the flesh is usually pink, tastes excellent and is not usually tainted with a muddy flavour. For a private fishery or syndicate, it would seem advisable to stock with equal numbers of brown and rainbow trout, thereby satisfying the preferences of all parties.

The terminology used for trout in the various stages of growth is a little confusing and is worth mentioning. The newly-hatched fish with its yolk sac is called an alevin or, in the U S A, a 'sac-fry'. In its first year the trout is called a fry or fingerling or a (0+fish). In its second year it is a yearling or a (1+fish): in its third year, a two-year old or (2+fish) and so on.

If for any reason, the owner is unable to make the necessary leasing arrangements and the lake is ready for stocking, he might well consider introducing say 500 fingerlings which would be of a catchable size by the next season. Mortality among fingerlings is likely to be higher than for larger trout, owing to predation by gulls and herons, and this must be taken into account. The cost of fingerlings is approximately half that of fish normally stocked.

Trout are sold by length rather than by weight and are usually introduced as two-year olds when 9 to 10in (22.9 to 25.4cm) long, their average weight being less than 0.5lb (227.0gm). Some owners like to stock their lakes with fish that are three years old and weigh about 2.2lb (1kg). The cost of fishing such water would be adjusted accordingly.

The rate of growth among trout in rivers and lakes varies widely even when there is a plentiful supply of food. When introduced from the fish farm, some fish are slightly larger than others. The larger fish pick the best feeding grounds in an established lake and drive away the smaller ones. The result is that some trout grow very fast and may increase their weight by 1kg during the months from May to October. The smaller trout may increase their weight by only 0.5kg or less. If, at the end of a fishing season, all the trout are not much bigger than when first put in, it is likely that the water has been overstocked in relation to the food supply and the only solution is to take out perhaps half the stock and transfer them elsewhere.

The fish will arrive in tanks in which there is a continuous flow of oxygen without which they would die in a very short time. The vehicle usually has a four-wheel drive to enable it to get as near to the water as possible; it is always necessary, however, to manhandle the fish into small containers such as plastic buckets and they should not be kept in the containers for more than a few minutes. A fisheries inspector, in some countries, will be present to ensure that all the fish look healthy.

The introduction of the fish into the water must be a gentle procedure. On no account should they be thrown in, as this will cause shock and bruising. A convenient and fairly deep part of the lake previously cleared of weed should be chosen, and each container should be lowered into the water and the trout allowed to swim out slowly so that they may adjust to the difference in water temperature. Most trout will swim off rapidly but a few may be torpid and flop over on their sides. When a fish flops on its side, its gills cannot work properly; it is advisable, therefore, to watch each batch for several minutes and any fish lying on the bottom must be gently put upright with the aid of a long rod. If this is done carefully there should be no casualties. Also any thick weed nearby must be cautiously prodded to see that no fish is caught up in it. It is said of brown trout that they are generally more vulnerable to travel and apt to bang their heads on the sides of the tank in which they are being transported. Rainbows do not have this habit and usually travel well.

During the first week after stocking, the lake margins should be checked for dead fish, but there should be none if they have been carefully handled. If a dead fish is discovered it must be removed to avoid polluting the water and examined superficially for any obvious cause of death such as external wounding.

Management

The successful management of a fishery involves a lot of work, both manual and written. If the owner is fortunate enough to have plenty of time and is a keen angler, he could perhaps manage a small concern. If he is a busy person, he would not have time to manage it efficiently and it would be advisable to let it to a syndicate on a long lease. This attracts a better price than a short lease because it gives security of tenure and makes it worth while for the syndicate to spend money on the fishery and maintain it to a high standard. The rental fees can be index-linked or subject to annual review. Short leases are generally much less attractive and less valuable.

There is seldom any difficulty in finding anglers who are prepared to pay what would seem to a non-angler to be very high prices for good trout fishing in pleasant surroundings. Although anglers are ready to pay well if the fishing is good, they will soon depart if the standard falls. In angling circles bad news soon gets around. Trout anglers, as a whole, are helpful, non-competitive people who will always tell a fellow angler where a good day's sport can be found as well as giving warning of places to avoid.

The efficient management of a fishery always calls for a set of regulations that differ from one fishery to another by reason of natural conditions. Such regulations are of benefit rather than a nuisance to the angler, because there will always be the mavericks who will insist on conducting things their own way. If this means taking three times their quota of fish on a day when fish are easily caught, then obviously it must be stopped.

A list of rules that also serves as an identification card should be issued to anyone authorised to fish the lake. There should be regulations covering the following points:

1. The dates of the fishing season, usually April 1 to September 30.
2. Fee must be paid before fishing begins.
3. All users must be in possession of a fishing licence, but a group or 'block' licence can be taken out by a syndicate, or in some cases by the owner of the fishery.
4. Liability for personal accident is the responsibility of the individual unless other arrangements are made.
5. The catch per day must be recorded, together with the date, size and type of fish and the bait used. A record book can be kept in a fishing hut or box, but sometimes this becomes too complicated in a small fishery and it is easier for each angler to make a monthly return of all fish caught. It is usually difficult to get anglers to submit records of the days when they catch nothing; this negative information, however, is extremely useful.
6. The number of days fishing allowed per week varies enormously. On some lakes, members have allotted days, on others they can fish every day of the week. Each system has its advantages and disadvantages.
7. A limit must be imposed on the number of fish caught per day or week, by each member.
8. The hours of fishing are usually from sunrise to sunset.
9. There must be strict rules about wading. Where there is mud, this can be dangerous and of no advantage to the angler. Indiscrimate

wading can do considerable damage to a fishery by disturbing the lakeside vegetation and submerged weed in which aquatic creatures live. It is therefore best prohibited.

10. Some fisheries have rules requiring all fish caught, regardless of size, to be kept; others insist that all undersized fish must be returned to the water. If a small fish is lightly hooked and carefully handled, it seems unreasonable not to put it back and, indeed, there have been instances where the same fish, with a marking on it, has been caught several times within a few days by the same angler.

    Most fish, caught on a fly, are hooked through the gristle of the jaws and suffer minimal damage, but if the hook gets deeper into the mouth, the damage caused is more serious and, if the fish is put back, it may just survive but is unlikely to gain weight.

11. Rules must be made about bringing guests to fish.

12. The type of bait to be used must be clearly defined. In some fisheries, when a new stock is put in, dry-fly fishing only is allowed for a week or so. Spinning is nearly always forbidden except perhaps at the end of the season.

13. Children and dogs must not be admitted because of the danger of them getting hooked up or tangled in the angler's line, quite apart from the disturbance they may cause.

The use of barbless hooks is becoming more popular, particularly in America. To land a fish by this method requires considerably more skill on the part of the angler and some fisheries make a rule that when a new batch of easily caught fish are first introduced into a lake, barbless hooks must be used for about two weeks. A trout which can get off these hooks suffers minimal damage to its mouth and will live to fight another day. Barbless hooks should therefore be encouraged but it is difficult to enforce their use.

The day-to-day expenses of running a trout fishery depend mainly on the size of the lake and whether it is necessary to employ someone as a part-time bailiff, which could be justified if there were 20 or so members, because the number of jobs that have to be done on the lake-side during the season are numerous. If they are not dealt with, fishing becomes difficult and anglers disgruntled. Control of lake-side vegetation is most important; if the lake-side assumes the appearance of a jungle, membership will fall.

Comfort may be considered by installing seats at intervals. Many anglers are elderly and they like somewhere to rest and something solid to put things on when changing a fly. Seats need not be elaborate – a wide board nailed on to four posts would be adequate.

There are many day-to-day chores such as cleaning sluices, removing dead fish, keeping a watch for signs of poachers and animal predators as well as disposing of excessive weed and keeping any footbridges in repair. This work is necessary if the fishery is to be maintained in good order and it would probably be necessary to employ someone part-time. During the winter months, only general supervision of the lake and its environment need be carried out, so some scheme whereby a person's working time could be reduced might be arranged.

There are no hard and fast rules about re-stocking. Stock should be maintained at a level sufficient to give the maximum amount of sport and therefore a close watch must be kept on the number of fish being caught so that roughly the same number can be replaced. In very hot weather it is advisable to slow down the rate of stocking until cooler weather returns.

The number of fish remaining at the end of the season should be as low as possible to prevent financial loss due to natural wastage and pre-dation by herons, cormorants and other fish-eating birds. Many angling clubs expect to recover about half or even two-thirds of the stocked fish during the season, depending on the intensity of fishing. It has been found by tagging fish that those that are not caught in the first year form an insignificant part of the catch in subsequent years.

A new scheme for use in large commercial fisheries is to have a floating cage in the lake to act as a stock-holding pen for fish where they can be held and fed until required. This is a scheme that could be adopted for smaller lakes; it consists of a circular cage of scaffolding, including a fitted walk-way made from galvanized steel tubing and floating on inflatable buoys. The whole structure is anchored to the lake bottom by three ropes attached to heavy concrete blocks placed in appropriate positions to counteract drift. The cage must be in the deepest part of the lake, well away from the shore and accessible only by boat. A cone-shaped net about 3.5m deep is suspended inside the circular walk-way, at least 1m clear of the bottom, to allow the escape of waste; the net can be quite easily raised for netting out fish. However, the use of the cage would be limited if there is insufficient depth and where there are high summer water temperatures causing reduced oxygen content. Another disadvantage is that trout outside in the lake would tend to congregate round the net because of the attraction of any surplus food. But the advantages are obvious: if the daily catch is recorded, that number of fish can be released into the lake, thus keeping the number constant and providing the angler with the maximum possible sport.

Financial savings could be made by buying small fish and bringing them on to a catchable size. Haulage costs can be greatly reduced and, most important of all, stocking with batches of fish already adapted to their surroundings, at regular intervals, avoids the introduction of a large number of easily-caught fish farm trout, thereby making for a fairer distribution of sport.

Information concerning holding cages can be obtained from the journals on trout farming such as 'Fish Farmer'. It is possible to construct a cage cheaply at home, providing one is able to secure accurate details of building. It must be emphasized that such cages cannot be used unless there is sufficient depth of water, ie about 5m.

A lake owner may consider letting out his fishing on a day-ticket system. Unless the anglers are known to him personally as people who respect the rules, such a move is not wise and constant supervision – as in a 'put-and-take' fishery – would be necessary. Almost inevitably under such a system there will be those who fish very successfully with worms, and, if caught, will plead ignorance. Such people should be barred from the fishery.

It is not possible to quote any accurate figures on the cost of building a lake or of running it as a trout fishery owing to a worldwide increase in the cost of labour, fish food and fish, but it is safe to say that the owner of a well-managed and well-stocked lake in pleasant surroundings will not only be able eventually to recover his initial costs but will be able to make a reasonable annual profit. Moreover, a waiting list of anglers only too keen to pay the price asked will develop.

At present there is a very small margin of profit for the producer of trout who sells for food consumption, because of limited public demand. If it were widely known that trout flesh is not only tasty and very nourishing, and gives all-round value for money, perhaps more people would want to eat it. With the present depletion and high price of sea fish in some countries, it may now find a more favourable market.

The spawning bed
It cannot be expected that a spawning bed will produce sufficient fish to

maintain the stock of brown trout needed in a fishery, but it will provide a few wild fish which will test the angler's skill. It is also of great interest to watch the spawning activities and to note the number and size of fish.

The size of the gravel stones is important. If they are too big, the trout may have difficulty in scraping out a depression in which to lay her eggs. If they are too small, the free flow of well-oxygenated water, so essential for the hatching out of the spawn, will be impeded. Each stone should be about 2–3cm in diameter. If the bed of the supply stream is rocky, the gravel may be put down on top of it, but if it is soft, a layer of black polythene should be laid to prevent the growth of weed which may clog the gravel by collecting silt.

Spawning usually starts in November in the northern hemisphere and continues for about twelve weeks. In the antipodes, trout have an annual growth rate and maturity cycle like trout in the northern hemisphere. They grow fastest in December and spawn in June and August. On the equator, as in Kenya, where breeding conditions are favourable all the year round, trout only breed once a year.

A pair of breeding trout will usualy complete their spawning activities within two or three weeks. A brood fish of 1kg in weight will lay about 1,500 to 2,000 eggs which are deposited in the depression she has dug for herself in the gravel. The male fish, waiting nearby, fertilizes the eggs as soon as they are laid. The eggs adhere to the gravel and the female moves forward a little, digging another depression and at the same time flicking the gravel backwards to cover up her first batch of eggs. Each spawning area or 'redd' may thus consist of a number of 'nests'. Within three or four months the eggs will hatch out and, provided there is an ample flow of water, the fry will remain in the spawning area until they are about fingerling size. If the supply of water is insufficient, they will move down into the lake.

In the wild state, the destruction of eggs and alevins in the first six months after laying is enormous. In the second and third year the losses are less but still high. Obviously it is important to prevent disturbance of the spawning area as far as possible from the end of October onwards for six months, otherwise ducks and other aquatic birds will eat the spawn and herons may attack the spawning fish.

When the supply stream is small, 1 or 2m wide and fairly shallow, spawning trout are unlikely to attempt to go further upstream as they would in a larger river and will probably be content with the area over which gravel has been spread. This area should be covered over with plastic netting as shown in *Fig 35*. The metal bar will not be completely effective in keeping out moorhens, grebes and ducks because they may dive under it, but as soon as the spawning season finishes at about the end of February the bar can be let right down to the bed of the stream and anchored there with stones.

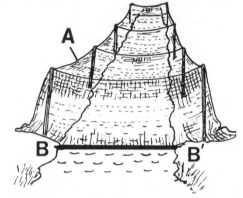

Fig 35   Spawning bed in a supply
   stream
A   – plastic netting
BB' – metal bar to hold netting
     down to water level

If the river supplying the lake is quite large, there is every possibility that trout, moving up out of the lake to spawn, will go a long way upstream and will be taken by poachers or predators. To prevent this upstream movement in the spawning season, a fish screen should be erected. In the author's experience on a millstream of the Hampshire Rother in the U K, a screen such as shown in *Fig 36* will serve the purpose well.

Cut the required length of stiff galvanized wire A of about 4cm square mesh, with a width sufficient to reach to the bottom of the stream, leaving a height of about 0.5m above the surface of the water. Before fixing this across the stream, a similar length of chicken wire B about

Fig 36   Cutaway view of spawning
   cage and fish screen
A   – galvanized fish screen
B   – chicken wire weighted down
     with stones
C   – covering of chicken wire
D   – gravel
E   – direction of flow
FF' – plastic floating pipe
G   – supporting bar

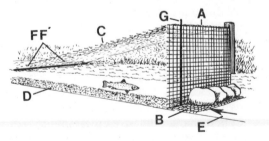

0.3m wide is firmly wired all along the bottom of the galvanized wire. When in position in the stream, the chicken wire is bent at a right angle

62

and heavy stones are placed upon it to block any gap under the fish screen. If this is not done, trout will burrow under the screen and escape upstream.

When the screen has been fixed across the stream it is then absolutely essential to prevent the trout from jumping over the top. They can easily clear 0.5m and they do this by taking a few preliminary jumps to gauge the height of the screen before they take a final leap over. To prevent the trout escaping in this way, the gravel bed must be roofed over with more chicken wire C attached along the top of the screen and sloped down to water level over a distance of about 4m above the gravel bed — the sides must also be filled in. The wire roof so formed will serve two purposes; it will keep out predators and waterfowl and will prevent the escape of trout ready to spawn. Such fish would be unable to get through a 4cm square mesh screen.

The end of the sloping wire forming the roof of the cage comes down in contact with the surface of the stream at FF', and this can be attached to a metal bar across the stream or preferably to a length of polythene pipe, corked at both ends, to make it float, thereby adjusting itself to any rise or fall in river level.

It is inevitable that, in the relatively small spawning area described above, there is considerable competition for space in which to lay eggs, and many eggs, carefully covered up by a previous spawning female, may be dug up again but in spite of this, as the author found, quite a number hatch out to become fingerling size in the following summer.

The screen must of course be kept clear of debris or any obstruction which might interfere with the flow of the stream. Movable screens, made in a similar fashion to that shown in *Fig 30*, but wider and not so high, are very useful for quick clearing of the screen.

4
Food of trout

The trout is carnivorous: that is to say, it feeds on aquatic animals and smaller fish living in the weed and mud at the bottom of a lake or river, as well as on lake flies. It will also eat non-aquatic insects such as moths, flies, caterpillars and leatherjackets falling onto the surface of the water. The trout swallows its prey whole, and though it has many small teeth, including some on the roof of its mouth, it only uses these for gripping its prey before devouring it. Food is completely digested in the stomach before it passes into the intestine. Trout belong to the so-called 'voracious' group of fishes of which the pike is the best example. This means that with very few exceptions, only prey that moves is eaten.

The evidence that trout are members of the so-called voracious group has been obtained by examination of many trout stomachs by survey teams. Anglers should make an occasional inspection of the stomach contents of fish they catch and this can be done with quite good results by using an instrument similar to a small salt spoon affixed to a 10cm handle. The instrument, usually called a 'marrow spoon', is passed into the stomach and the contents scooped out and inspection of what the trout has been feeding on can help anglers in the choice of artificial flies. A fuller examination requires the removal of the stomach and the emptying of the contents into a glass container and dilution with water. Usually quite a wide variety of aquatic insects and invertebrates, ranging from shrimps, snails, beetles and nymphs to very small gnat larvae and daphnia will be revealed. Occasionally there is some weed mixed in with the food but it is generally agreed that a trout swallows this unintentionally along with the animal it catches.

In a river, a trout will find a place in the stream to its liking and will stay there awaiting the arrival of small aquatic animals carried down by the current and it watches for flies floating on the surface of the water.

Occasionally it will forage for snails or other slow-moving animals.

In fish farms, young and adult trout are fed on specially manufactured pellets which are described in more detail later. Under artificial conditions trout have adapted themselves to feeding on non-living food but as soon as they are put into a lake or river, they very soon become accustomed to finding their natural food.

Trout often feed around beds of weed where the aquatic life is richest and, in a lake, this is likely to be within 30m from the shoreline. When feeding actively they tend to be more selective in their choice of food and concentrate on the one particular type of fly or nymph which is most abundant. The probable reason for this selectivity is that the trout finds it more economical to make the same movements repeatedly in snatching its prey, rather than varying each movement for different types of animal: this is why an angler often becomes so frustrated when all around him fish are feeding actively but he is unable to get a 'touch'. If it can be discovered what the trout are taking (which is by no means easy) and the appropriate imitation is available to fix to the end of the line, successful fishing will be achieved until the trout suddenly decide to change to some other form of fly, which happens quite often.

There is a natural tendency to think that trout are not feeding unless they are rising to catch insects on the surface of the water. The reverse is often true, because trout get most of their food from animals living below the surface.

In spring and summer they spend much of their time in mid-water, hunting nymphs as they rise to the surface to hatch out. Lake flies and non-aquatic insects such as moths, caterpillars and leatherjackets falling on the water also form part of the trout's diet in the summer months; it is during these months that increase in weight occurs. During the winter months, they continue to feed but their digestion is slower and therefore they eat less and hardly put on any weight.

It is important to the angler to have a basic knowledge of the more common lake flies and to be able to identify them; in addition, some knowledge about the many animals living on the lake bottom and providing the main food for trout should be acquired. The various forms of aquatic life found in fresh water, upon most of which the trout feeds, are listed below.

Lake flies and their aquatic forms
    Mayflies (Ephemeroptera)

Stoneflies (Plecoptera)
Caddis flies (Trichoptera)
Alder flies (Megaloptera)
Midges and black flies (Diptera)
Damselflies and dragonflies (Odonata)
Crustaceans
Daphnia (Cladocera)
Freshwater shrimp (*Gammarus pulex)*
Water-louse (*Asellus aquaticus*)
Molluscs
Snails, limpets, mussels
Worms
Bristle worms, tubifex, earthworms and leeches
Water beetles (Coleoptera)
Water bugs (Hemiptera)
Rotifers
Small fish

Mayflies (Ephemeroptera)

Mayflies, sometimes called dayflies because they only live for a day, are very important for the angler on chalk streams and quite important for lake fisheries, but it is not within the scope of this book to describe the many species of mayfly which can vary in size from 4–16mm (*Fig 37*).

The fascinating life cycle of the mayfly has four stages. Starting as an egg, after a short period depending on water temperature, a tiny nymph or larva hatches out and begins feeding on particles of algae on the lake or river bottom. As it grows bigger, it has to shed its skin several times until it reaches maturity as a nymph (*Fig 37*, A). This second stage usually takes about two years in the case of mayflies.

The nymph then either crawls up a weed stem or swims to the surface where, after a brief period, the skin splits down its back and it emerges rapidly into what is called the sub-imago or dun (*Fig 37*, B). The dun then flies to the bank where it takes cover among the vegetation until such time as it is ready to undergo its final metamorphosis into an adult spinner (*Fig 37*, C). This final stage may take place after a period of minutes or it may be prolonged for a day or two, depending on the weather.

The fourth stage as a spinner is very brief. If it is a female spinner it will hide itself in vegetation. If a male, it will join together with other

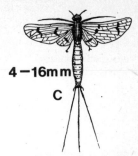

Fig 37
A – nymph of mayfly
B – dun or sub-imago
C – adult spinner

A   B   C

4 – 16mm

8 – 24mm

males in the aerial dance over the water so often seen by anglers in the evening. The female spinners, attracted by this male display, join the dance but are immediately seized by a male and aerial fertilization takes place.

After fertilization, the female lays her eggs either by dropping them in the water or by dipping on to the surface of the water. After all the eggs are laid, the female collapses on the water as a 'spent spinner' and the males drift off either to die on the surface of the water or inland.

It can be seen that in all four stages of development the mayfly is very vulnerable to the trout and the latter is quick to take advantage. The amazing speed with which a swimming nymph can convert itself into a weakly flying 'dun' on the surface of the water is miraculous but it is not always quick enough to avoid the sharp-eyed trout.

The mayfly prefers alkaline water and most chalk streams have a large population but they will live also in muddy streams and lakes. Being very weak fliers, they are unlikely to find their way into a newly-made lake unless it is very close to a well-established breeding place and it is therefore necessary to introduce nymphs from elsewhere. This can be easily done using a close-meshed fishing net and working it lightly among the water weed of a stream. Nymphs not only of mayflies but of other lake flies will be caught. Snails, shrimps and water-slaters (*Fig 44*) should all be added to the catch.

Stoneflies (Plecoptera)
The various species of this lake fly provide a source of trout food mainly from the nymphs which, as the name suggests, live among the stones in the bed of the river or lake. Trout take the nymphs as they crawl along the bottom on their way to the bank where they hatch into adult flies. The only opportunity the trout gets to catch an adult stonefly is when the female lays her eggs on the water.

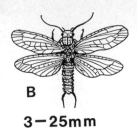

Fig 38
A — nymph of stonefly
B — adult

3 — 25mm

Sedge or caddis fly (Trichoptera)

These flies, of which there are many species, are of considerable importance as trout food. The life cycle consists of four stages: egg, larva, pupa and adult. The larval stage is when most species build around themselves the well-known protective case of little stones and debris (*Fig 39*, A). When the larva is mature, it goes into the pupal stage like a chrysalis (*Fig. 39*, B). From this it eventually emerges as an adult sedge or caddis fly (*Fig 39*, C). Trout feed on the larvae and pupae, eating the case as well, and on newly-hatched adult flies and on females as they lay their eggs. The adult sedge is usually grey or grey-brown in colour and the rather furry appearance of the wings makes it look not unlike a moth.

It is worth mentioning that there is often some confusion between the words larva and nymph. They both represent the same stage in growth, but the nymph is so called because it bears a recognizable likeness to the adult fly.

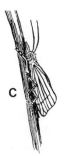

Fig 39
A — larva of sedge or caddis fly
B — pupa
C — adult

8 — 22mm   **10 — 30mm**

Alder flies (Megaloptera)

These flies are commonly seen in early summer by the waterside. They are brown in colour and could be mistaken for sedge flies but their wings have dark vein-like markings and are devoid of hairs. They are not truly aquatic insects because only part of their life cycle is spent in the water. The eggs are laid on bank vegetation and when the larvae hatch, they crawl into the water where they remain for about a year until ready for pupation which takes place in the mud of the bank. It is during the larval stage that they form quite an important food for the trout. The adult flies are not generally favoured by trout (*Fig 40*).

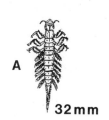

Fig 40
A – larva of alder fly
B – adult

A

B

32mm   20 – 30mm

Midges (Diptera)

There are very many species in this group and they can usually be seen throughout the warm weather by every waterside. They form an important part of the diet of lake trout.

The life cycle of the midge consists of four stages: egg, larva, pupa and adult. The eggs are laid on the water and when the larvae hatch out they bury themselves in the mud or hide in weed. When mature they pupate (*Fig 41*). The pupae can swim and when ready to hatch into adult flies, they swim up, suspend themselves to the under-surface of the water for a brief period before hatching into adults. It is at this stage that the trout catch them.

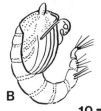

Fig 41
A – larva of midge
B – pupa

A   B

10 –20mm

Black gnats (*Biblio johannis*)

These flies are very familiar to anglers and are usually seen swarming over the water about midsummer though they can be seen earlier. They fall on the water in large numbers and are eagerly taken by trout of all sizes. The adult fly has shiny wings and is about 7mm long. Though it is called 'black', it is actually a dark olive in colour.

Damselflies (Zygoptera), Dragonflies (Anisoptera)
Large swarms of damselflies often appear on the waterside during summer. They measure about 40mm long and may be purple, blue, green or red in colour, and occasionally they are eaten by trout both in their nymphal and adult forms (*Fig 42*). Damselflies look like miniature dragonflies, the latter being three or four times bigger than damsels and neither they, nor their nymphs, are eaten by trout. The dragonfly nymph with its formidable, pincer-like jaws, is a very unwelcome visitor where there are small fish; it is about 5cm in length and of a grey-brown colour.

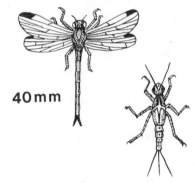

Fig 42   Damselfly and nymph   **40mm**

30mm

Crustaceans
Crustaceans form a very large group and they are a most important source of food, both for adult fish and trout fingerlings. The lower crustacean group includes daphnia (Cladocera) (*Fig 43*), very small primitive creatures about 1.5mm to 3.0mm in length, and although they are so minute, trout are said to catch them one at a time rather than filter them through their mouths.

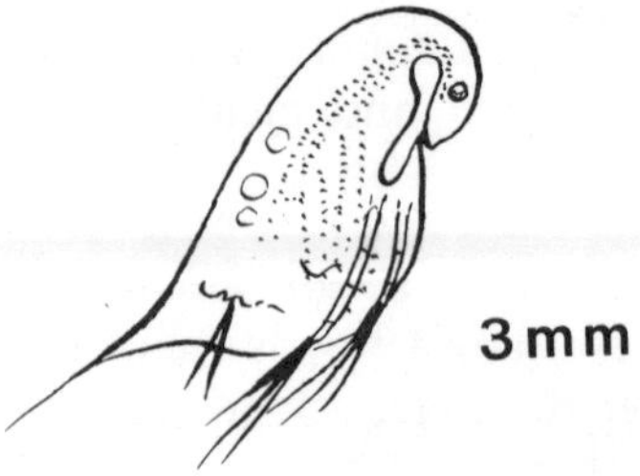

Fig 43   Daphnia or water flea

3mm

Of the higher crustacean group, the freshwater shrimp (*Gammarus pulex*) is the commonest and most important and, together with the water-louse or slater (*Assellus aquaticus*) (*Fig 44*), the next most common, they form a major part of the trout's diet during the winter months, particularly in lakes; they also contribute largely to the pink colour of trout flesh. Shrimps breed very rapidly in the right conditions but to ensure a good supply in a newly-made lake, as many as possible should be introduced from another source. Both these crustaceans feed on weed and rotting vegetation on the bottom of the lake or river.

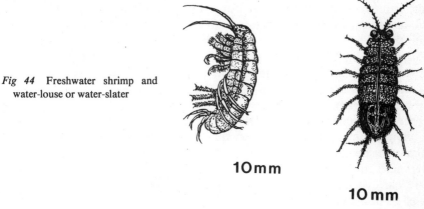

Fig 44 Freshwater shrimp and water-louse or water-slater

10mm

10 mm

Molluscs
This group comprises freshwater snails, limpets, sea mussels and freshwater mussels (trout will only eat the small type of mollusc). A stock of snails should be put into a newly-made lake and this is usually quite a simple task as they can be found easily, feeding in large numbers on weed, especially in chalk streams.

Worms
The trout eats three groups of aquatic worms: the bristle worm, which is transparent and measures about 60 to 80mm in length; the tubifex worm, reddish in colour and varying in length from 8 to 80mm; and lastly, the flatworm, a flattish grey worm living among stones and mud on the bottom (leeches belong to this group but are rarely eaten by fish). The tubifex makes a kind of tube for itself from mud particles that it sinks into the ground; the anterior end of its body stays within the tube

71

while the tail waves about in the water to secure particles of food; it forms large colonies where mud is plentiful and it is usually the first living creature to appear in water recovering from pollution. Earthworms are readily consumed by trout when they find them. After heavy rain, they are sometimes washed by an inflowing stream into a lake where trout are ready waiting for them.

Trout invariably grow very well during the first year after their introduction into a newly-established lake. The reason for this is not clear; it could be due to the number of earthworms and other non-aquatic creatures they can find or that the water is free from parasites, but it seems more likely that being all roughly of the same age and size, the trout have no established peck order among themselves. There are no large trout, with which they would have to compete for food, occupying the lake. It is generally accepted by trout breeders that a number of large trout in the same water with smaller ones will slow down the growth of the latter, even though there may be an abundance of food.

Water beetles (Coleoptera)
There are numerous species of diving beetle and as they are all capable of flying, they find their way very quickly to a new lake. Trout will sometimes eat the smaller adult beetles, but they rarely touch the larvae. The larvae of the bigger beetles, particularly that of the great diving beetle, are carnivorous and will attack small trout larger than themselves, as well as destroying many fry.

Water bugs (Hemiptera)
Water bugs, such as the water boatman, pond skater, water cricket and others, all make an appearance soon after a lake has been filled. Apart from the water boatman (which swims upside down), they are not eaten by trout; in fact, they compete vigorously with trout fry for food.

Rotifers
These are extremely small creatures (*Fig 45*) found in great numbers feeding on the rich vegetable matter and plankton on the lake bottom. They provide an important source of food not only for fry and small fish but also for the aquatic animals upon which larger fish feed.

Small fish
Generally trout, under natural conditions, will only become cannibalistic

Fig 45   Rotifers

1mm   1mm

or piscivorous when they have attained a certain age and size, but this cannot be taken as a general rule. Some large trout are found to have a very mixed diet in their stomachs, whereas some smaller ones can be shown to have been mainly piscivorous.

Trout fry crowded together under artificial conditions may become cannibalistic, especially where there is a difference in their size and if, in a hatchery, one tray floods over in to another one, containing different sized fry, the larger fry will eat the smaller ones.

Trout that have become piscivorous will eat sticklebacks, minnows, small perch, small trout, salmon, elvers, bullheads and loach. Fish swimming in shoals, such as minnows and sticklebacks, are taken more often than non-shoaling fish. All these small fish compete with trout for food and introducing them into a trout lake would not be prudent. On the other hand, it could be argued that there is always a small percentage of trout evading capture, growing old and big, which eventually develop piscivorous tendencies and they would certainly eat small trout if there were no other species of fish in the lake for them to eat.

Feeding habits of trout

Depending on the water temperature in the stream, the trout egg, in the natural state, hatches in a gravel bed between March and May. The young fry stays in the gravel until its yolk sac is fully absorbed; it then emerges and takes up a position where the current is not too strong, and facing upstream it starts feeding on small aquatic animals drifting towards it. Other fry, each having its own established territory, station themselves alongside. This habit of waiting for food to be brought down by the current remains throughout the life of trout living in streams. In lakes, where there is little or no current, trout have to search for food but they still have their own particular territory which they try to defend. If flooding of a lake occurs, many terrestrial creatures such as earthworms,

73

grasshoppers and leatherjackets may be seen in the water. The trout change greedily to a diet of these creatures, even when there is a plentiful supply of their normal food available.

It is generally accepted that trout grow faster where the water is hard as, for example, in chalk streams. Their growth in soft or acid water tends to be much slower. The reason for this difference in the rate of growth is that where water contains dissolved calcium exceeding 150ppm as calcium carbonate, the conditions for weed growth are much more favourable and abundant weed is essential for the aquatic creatures the trout feed upon.

Artificial feeding

As soon as the young fry are able to feed themselves, they are given a mixture of finely pulped ox spleen, brains or sea fish, sometimes with finely ground-up cooked shrimps to which about 3% yeast is added for vitamin content. The mixture is put into the breeding trays and forms a cloud of small particles in the water to which the fry help themselves; the uneaten residue sinks to the bottom through fine mesh wire and is so washed away in the constantly flowing stream of water.

When the trout reach the fingerling stage, they are fed on very small dried pellets comprising about 50% protein from animal waste, 40% carbohydrate and a small percentage of fats, minerals and vitamins. Yearling trout or 1+fish (about 15cm long) are fed on slightly larger pellets roughly the size of a small garden pea, consisting of the same materials; such pellets form their basic diet until the fish are sold from the hatchery. The price of these dry concentrates is high and waste should be eliminated as far as possible. They must be stored in a dry place for no longer than six months, otherwise the vitamin content deteriorates.

Lake feeding

The lake owner need not be concerned with the finer technicalities of feeding trout in order to produce the maximum rate of growth, and pellets should only be used for a short period when a new stock of fish is settling in and has not adjusted to finding natural food.

Feeding should be at the rate of about ten handfuls per 100 fish, three times a week for three or four weeks. The pellets will float for about six hours and, obviously, if there is a wind, they must always be thrown with the wind behind them so that they float across the lake and become widely distributed. If this precaution is not adopted, they will collect along the shore line and be wasted or attract vermin, and also expose the trout to attack by herons.

Sinking pellets are now available and the advantage of using them is that there is no chance of them drifting to the shoreline. It is advisable to throw the pellets in the parts of the lake where there is least mud to avoid wastage, but trout usually congregate around the feeding areas and are quick to catch most of the sinking pellets in midwater. They do not disturb the surface of the water to any extent so that it is difficult to estimate how many are feeding in one particular spot. When feeding on floating pellets, trout will readily show themselves, giving the owner a good idea of their size and numbers, so that both kinds of pellets have their advantages.

Winter feeding, if the weather is mild, is advisable. The owner should use his discretion as to the amount of food dispersed. If there is an active response and the trout seem to be hungry, he can give them as much as they want, but if the pellets are not immediately taken, it means that the trout are getting a sufficient supply of food from the bottom or that for one reason or another, the stock of trout has greatly diminished.

Some anglers will say that trout once put into a lake should find their natural food and ought not to be fed, otherwise they become poor sport fish. Whether this theory is valid or not is difficult to say, since it is a fact that although trout do not increase their weight during winter months, they nevertheless continue to feed, though less actively. It is generally accepted that they are in better condition in early spring if they have had winter feeding than if they had not.

When a lake is well stocked with trout and yet anglers are catching fewer fish than would be expected, it is advisable to see if the fish caught are in good condition with a good pink coloration of the flesh. If this proves to be the case and it is observed that fish do not seem to rise freely when there is a good hatch of fly, then it is very likely that the fish are gorging themselves on shrimps and snails.

If, on inspection of the shallows, large numbers of shrimps are found and many snails in the weed, it is clear that there is too much natural feed in the lake for the number of fish present and the stock must therefore be increased. Conversely, if the fish are easily caught but are of very much the same size as they were when introduced into the lake, it is more than likely there is insufficient food available. This could also happen in a lake with very good spawning facilities where a large population of small trout could create a shortage of food.

It is always of interest to the angler to know the times of the day when trout feed most actively, as it is the general experience that there are slack periods when it is almost a waste of time to fish. This is because trout need sufficient light in order to see their prey. During the shorter days they may feed continuously, but in spring and summer, if there is plenty of food available, they will sometimes stop feeding for a time; a slack period often occurs about mid-day till late afternoon. They are then in the habit of continuing to feed on and off until dusk.

There is one thing which is certain and that is that trout are most capricious in their feeding habits and that there are no hard and fast rules as to feeding times. Even on a warm, calm evening with ideal conditions on the water, an angler may return home with an empty bag.

5
Enemies of trout

The trout's most dangerous enemy, of course, is man. A hatchery-born trout is comparatively tame but, as soon as it is put into a lake or river, it quickly learns that a man on the bank spells the worst kind of danger. This fear is probably transmitted by the wild trout already present in the water rather than by any inherited factor, because trout reared artificially, like most fish, can become almost finger tame and remain so as long as they are kept in captivity.

Poachers
Poaching of edible fish is now very prevalent and, with the continually rising price of food, it is likely to increase and become a popular means of supplementing income and the larder. Poachers' main targets are trout farms where there are large concentrations of valuable fish. Most farms in the past have suffered heavy losses but present-day security measures have made such poaching much more difficult. However, small private and commercial fisheries are still liable to attack and especially so if poachers are able to find out when lakes have been freshly stocked.

The main poaching methods used are:

1. Several lines with floats are baited with worms or maggots. Fish are attracted to the area by trout pellets, similar to those on which they have been fed in the fish farm, being thrown into the water. If a poacher is skilful and the trout are 'on the feed', at least a dozen fish could be caught in the space of one hour by such a method. Rods are not often used as they are too difficult to conceal.
2. The use of nets is not popular; it is a cumbersome method and if poachers are caught unawares the evidence is difficult to dispose of.

It is most unlikely that they would try netting a lake, even if they had a boat, because the risk would far outweigh the catch, but a net placed across a well-stocked, medium-sized river could be well worthwhile, the fish being driven towards it by somebody wading in the stream. Poaching a fish farm, however, where the risk is high but the reward great, would almost certainly involve the use of nets, unless the stock ponds could be emptied rapidly and the fish taken out with hand nets.

3. Setting night lines baited with worms is a method employed by poachers who have little time to spare during the day. The use of a night line is a wretched way of catching trout which may remain on the hook – often a double or treble one – for 24 hours or more. Night lines are difficult to detect if they are carefully laid, but the occasional use of drag line and hook along a lake margin will soon reveal what is happening. An old country method used to 'foul hook' a big fish which can be seen lying under a river bridge is to set rows of hooks on a loop of line. The loop of hooks is carefully worked round the fish from behind and the line is pulled up sharply, hooking the body of the victim. This scheme could be used in a trout lake by throwing the hooks 'blind' amongst a good concentration of fish feeding vigorously on trout pellets, but it would be hit-or-miss and the methods of the modern poacher are usually much more sophisticated.

4. Poisoning, sometimes used in rivers, is the most despicable form of poaching. It would be ineffective in lakes as the current is insufficient to spread the poison quickly. The poison used has a cyanide base and is reputed not to make the flesh unfit for human consumption, but it is hard to believe that many people would care to eat a fish so killed, if they were aware of the method of its death. If used in a river such a poison rapidly kills every form of life in the water for a long way downstream until it becomes so diluted as to be rendered harmless.

There is a story about poaching that involves a less lethal type of poison. A water bailiff in a concealed position on a well-known trout river was watching a man on the opposite bank steadily scooping out live trout from the water with a long-handled net. The bailiff, who thought he knew all the poaching tricks, was at a complete loss to understand what was going on until he looked upstream where he saw a man leaning idly on a bridge, watching the stream. Becoming suspicious, he decided to find out what the man was doing and, like all bailiffs, he possessed that very disturbing habit of appearing from nowhere and came up to the man quietly and discovered that he was feeding the trout with wasp grubs pickled in gin, making the fish so drunk that they were incapable of swimming against the current and so falling an easy prey to the man's accomplice downstream.

5. Wet suits with spear guns are sometimes used in big pools where there are salmon or large trout but it is unlikely that such a method would be used for catching lake trout.

6. Explosives are still used in remote areas but only in salmon pools. They would not be used on a lake unless the poachers had a boat with which to pick up the fish. Risk of detection is high and the method is not without danger.

7. Stunning by electricity is a method frequently used on fish farms for the collection of brood trout or by Water Authorities for clearing out unwanted fish. It requires the use of a generator or batteries with two insulated cables carrying a current of about $1\frac{1}{2}$ amperes to the poles. Direct current is safer to use, where the fish are attracted to the positive pole from around which they can be scooped out after they have been temporarily stunned. The equipment required is necessarily heavy and cumbersome and must be used in daylight by a reasonably skilled operator. Except in most favourable circumstances, it would seem, therefore, to be a very risky way of poaching fish.

Trout poaching has reached such proportions that all fish farmers and owners of large fisheries, particularly those located near towns, take full precautionary measures against such predacity.

Fencing with barbed wire or chain link is essential and the more formidable the fence the better.

Guard dogs, preferably two or three animals of the same breed, are absolutely necessary in large establishments and they must be allowed to roam freely within the boundary. Instinctively, dogs will hunt as a pack and as such they are much more effective than a lone animal; moreover, poachers have a technique for dealing with a solitary dog.

Floodlighting is usually a routine installation on trout farms in case of night floods or other emergencies; it also acts as a strong deterrent. On a small fishery it would probably be uneconomic.

Many ingenious electric alarm systems, activated by somebody walking on a concealed flat surface, are available but very expensive. A simple and effective warning method is a tripwire apparatus attached to a loud clanging, well-concealed bell which is particularly useful on a dark night. When the owner has himself inadvertently tripped over the wire several times during the day, he will realize what a shattering effect such a device could have on the nerves of any poacher on a quiet night.

If poachers or other unwelcome predators are suspected of visiting a trout lake, a simple way to find out is to have several patches of raked sand at intervals around the lake-side, not forgetting to warn authorized persons to avoid them. Such patches, even if they reveal no human footprints, often show interesting signs of wild life and the information can be very useful.

A boat on a lake of any size is necessary for such purposes as the removal of debris, weed cutting or weed spraying, in addition to angling. When the boat is not in use it must be securely padlocked and the oars and rollocks removed and hidden away.

Some lakes in low-lying country may have a simple iron grid system at their outflows in order to prevent fish escaping downstream; if the grid is not securely fixed or padlocked into position, a poacher, sooner or later, will remove it, allowing fish to swim into water where he can deal with them more easily.

In these unsettled times it is a wise precaution to approach poachers with care and not by oneself; either inform the police or seek the help of one or two strong men as witnesses, otherwise it will be almost impossible to confiscate their gear and press a formal charge.

Animals

The mink

The mink is perhaps the worst of all predators where trout are concerned. There are three types: Russian, European and North American and they vary in colour from light to very dark brown. It is well known that mink have escaped from various fur farms in the U K and have become well established in Devon, Somerset, Hampshire, West Sussex, Cumbria and East Anglia and, in spite of constant attempts to reduce their numbers, they still seem to be spreading. The mink which have escaped are usually dark brown and have a small white patch under their chins which is a distinguishing feature. They vary in length from 45cm to 60cm including the tail and are North American in origin.

A mink always lives near water, its favourite food being fish but it will eat rabbits, game and waterfowl of all kinds. It is a bold, vicious killer and an agile climber, but swimming and diving are its predominant skills. Hunting for trout in a lake, it will create panic among the fish — which have an instinctive fear of otter-like animals — and this renders the lake unfishable for a considerable time.

Whether a mink could outswim a fully-grown trout over a short distance is doubtful, because a trout can sprint very rapidly for about 30 seconds, but it then tires quickly; however, if a mink can succeed in driving its prey into shallow water, it has no difficulty in getting to grips with it.

The mink is a curious and inquisitive animal. It is not particularly frightened of man and many anglers have reported seeing them at very close range, apparently oblivious to the presence of humans. In one instance a mink actually stole a dead fish when the angler was only 10m away from it. Nevertheless, they are elusive creatures and never seem to establish themselves in one place for any length of time. They would be less of a menace to fisheries, poultry keepers and wild life in general if they killed only for their own needs but they appear to indulge their killer instinct for the sheer pleasure of it, and if they can find trout in a confined space such as a fish farm or get into a chicken-run, they will spread death and destruction. Wherever there are valuable fish stocks and there are wild mink present in the area, an attempt must be made to get rid of them. It is compulsory in the U K to report their presence to the Water Authority who try to control their numbers by trapping.

The trap, like a large wire-cage rat-trap, is set near to the water's edge, firmly pegged down and covered with dead grass; it is baited with fresh fish which must be tied into the end of the trap. A strong piece of cord should be attached to the trap so that it may be easily carried if a mink is caught. When trapped, mink are extremely vicious and make a fearsome noise. It is advisable to keep fingers well away. The animal should be shot in the trap with a 0.22 rifle or with a shot gun at about 20m range to avoid destroying the trap. Alternatively, it can be gassed by putting the trap into a plastic bag and placing the mouth of the bag over a car exhaust pipe. Drowning is inhumane, as mink are great underwater swimmers and take a long time to die. If, as is sometimes done, the trap is set under water, then the mink does drown.

A partly eaten, freshly killed fish near the water's edge, is likely to be the work of a mink. Their footprints (*Fig 46*) can sometimes be found in a muddy patch, and they differ from those of the otter in having no webbing imprint between the toes. Their excrement is dark and often contains bones and fish scales; usually it is deposited on top of a log or large stone.

The otter (*Lutra lutra*)

Otters, now rare, are no longer a problem to fisheries. Driven out of their usual haunts by persecution and specially by pollution, they can now be found only in the remoter parts of the world or in conservation areas, and should be given every encouragement to re-establish themselves.

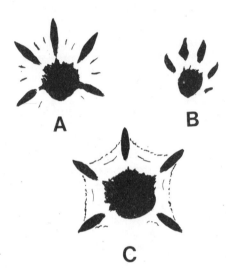

Fig 46   Footprints
A – mink
B – stoat
C – otter

The water shrew (*Neomys fodiens*)

This small, mouse-like creature about 10cm long, is a remarkably good swimmer and diver and when seen swimming under water, it has a silver appearance due to the retention of air bubbles within its fur. It is very destructive to trout eggs and fry and is therefore most unwelcome in trout hatcheries and spawning beds, but is otherwise harmless.

The water vole (*Arvicolina amphibius*)

The water vole, so often mistaken for a brown rat, is a complete vegetarian and is not a direct enemy of trout. It does, however, cause a considerable amount of trouble by undermining banks with its burrowings which can give rise to leaks. In trout farms, where there are often ponds with earth banks, it can create much havoc by digging holes from one pond to another through which the fish escape, thus allowing different sizes of fish to be mixed up. Terriers are the best solution to such a problem; they will also account for any brown rats which frequently take over the burrows and spread disease.

The coypu (*Myopotamus*)
This creature, a native of South America, is also a complete vegetarian always living near water. It was introduced to some countries for fur farming. Some escaped in the U K and have established themselves firmly in the eastern part of the country. It can cause considerable damage to root crops such as sugar beet. It digs large burrows in banks or dams where water is impounded and the resulting leaks can be serious.

Mink and coypus are two examples of non-native species having been introduced for financial gain into an environment where they have no natural enemies except man. Compared with their normal habitat, mink and coypus find an easy living in the U K, and, where food is abundant, it is a law of nature that large litters are produced. For both of these animals it is highly important that careful surveillance and strict control be exercised in order to restrict their numbers.

Birds

The heron (*Ardea cinerea*)
Of all the fish-eating birds the heron is generally regarded by fishery owners as the greatest nuisance, but it is by no means all bad, killing as it does many coarse fish, eels, frogs, water shrews, water voles, moles, rats and mice. In a coarse fishing lake the heron's activities could be said to be beneficial if the fish population is too high, as is very often the case.

In a trout lake a heron can do a lot of damage and it will regularly visit a well-stocked lake in the early morning and evening unless disturbed. For its size, it weighs very little, about 5lbs (2.25kg), but it eats surprisingly large meals and can swallow a fish as big as a medium-sized trout without any difficulty. It has the ability to vomit up the whole of its stomach contents if taken unawares, a tactic facilitating an easy take-off. If it catches a large fish, it will move it on to the bank and after repeated stabbings will consume it piecemeal. Unfortunately, a heron sometimes stabs a fish which is able to escape with a wound in its back, and such fish, bearing minor wounds which have healed and left the fish in good condition, are quite often caught by anglers; others, with deep wounds, would not survive.

Many ingenious methods have been employed for scaring herons away, such as scarecrows, automatic bangers, imitation herons and pieces of flapping grey cloth in the shape of a heron, but these are only effective for about a week and then something else must be tried. Things that move in the wind are generally more effective than immobile objects. A nesting pair of Canada geese or a pair of swans will keep herons away better than anything else during the breeding season for they know that herons will readily kill the newly-hatched young of all waterfowl.

Wire netting and strands of wire have been tried unsuccessfully in places where herons usually fish but these prove more of a nuisance to the angler than to the herons. Though they usually fish in shallow water, they sometimes wade in until their bodies are afloat and they can swim for short distances.

The various species of herons are widely distributed over Europe, Asia, Africa and America. In the U S A, U K and most European countries, herons are a protected species and it is an offence to kill one but this may be a law more honoured in the breech than the observance – one can sympathize with an enraged fish farmer when he sees a dozen herons helping themselves to his livelihood.

If herons are visiting a fishery, their footprints can invariably be seen in the mud of the shallows. They must not be confused with those of a moorhen which, for its size, leaves a large footprint (*Fig 47*). The distinguishing feature, apart from size, is that the imprint of the back claw of the heron is straight, whereas that of the moorhen deviates inwards.

The cormorant (*Phalacrocorax carbo*)

Cormorants are most unwelcome in a trout fishery. When not engaged in breeding activities, these sea birds fly far inland on fishing expeditions; they are a great menace and will soon reduce the trout population in a well-stocked lake. Not only do they kill many fish, consuming more than their own weight per day, but they create consternation and fear to such an extent that it would be a waste of time for an angler to try catching trout after a cormorant has been in action. On a large lake it is often difficult to detect the presence of these birds, partly because they spend a lot of time under water and also because they do not show themselves much above the water line except for their heads, so an inexperienced observer could confuse them with ducks. When they have finished

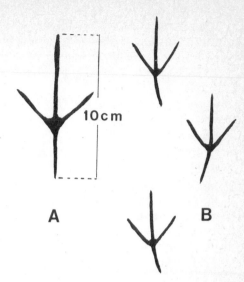

Fig 47 Footprints
A – heron
B – moorhen

10cm

A

B

diving, they can be clearly identified sitting on a post or rock and drying their wings, as they are the only web-footed bird with no natural waterproofing oil on its feathers.

The red-breasted merganser (*Mergus serrator*)
The goosander (*Mergus merganser*)
These gaily coloured ducks have long bills specially adapted for gripping their food. They have, perhaps undeservedly, got a reputation for catching large numbers of trout and young salmon but they do, in fact, get most of their food in the form of eels, crabs, shrimps, worms and other kinds of aquatic life. Because of persecution by water bailiffs, they are rarely seen in England but are fairly common in Scotland, Ireland and generally throughout the Northern Hemisphere.

The black-headed gull (*Larus ridibundus*)
The black-headed gull, somewhat misnamed because it has a chocolate coloured head during the breeding season only, is one of the smaller gulls but by far the most numerous. In common with most of its species, it is a scavenger. Flocks come far inland to congregate in urban areas where there are rubbish tips and it is surprising that they do not create pollution problems because they roost in their hundreds on large reservoirs. They will certainly take trout fry or fingerlings, but present a

greater danger to fish as carriers of disease on their feet and in their excreta, for they will feed indiscriminately on any dead or diseased fish, or offal. It is unwise, therefore, to allow these birds to roost on a trout lake and some system must be devised to scare them off.

The great black-backed gull (*Larus marinus*)

This large gull ranges over northern Europe, Greenland to the eastern seaboard of North America. It is a ferocious killer of the young of other sea birds and ducklings and, like all gulls, it will eat any form of offal. Fortunately, it does not fly very far inland, but if it discovers a well-stocked lake near the coast, it will cause much damage to the fish and wild life in general by picking up quite large trout swimming near the surface, or destroying the eggs and the young of waterfowl.

Other types of gulls keep more or less to the coastal regions and are less harmful, but it is prudent to discourage them all because of the danger of their transmitting disease.

The coot (*Fulica atra*)
The moorhen (*Gallinula chloropus*)

Moorhens and coots, particularly the latter, are very much a mixed blessing. Both will eat trout fry and spawn, when they can find it, and although a large part of their diet is made up of vegetable matter and water insects, they will also eat the eggs of waterfowl and any other birds nesting round the margin of the lake. During the breeding season coots become very quarrelsome and vicious, even attacking adult waterfowl. Too many coots on a fishery can be a nuisance to the angler by disturbing the water with their ceaseless fighting and splashing, their activities being carried on, as often as not, close to where the the angler is fishing.

The red-throated diver (*Colymbus stellatus*)
The great northern diver (*Colymbus immer*)
The black-throated diver (*Colymbus arcticus*)

These attractive but somewhat rare birds breed in the northern hemisphere but in the winter months move southwards to inland lakes and estuaries. They may well be seen on large fishing waters and reservoirs where they will certainly take small fish, but the harm they can do is very limited and on no account should they be persecuted.

86

There are other diving birds which may appear and actually breed on fishing waters. These are the grebes (Podicipidae). They are all natives of Europe and Asia and the Slavonic grebe is also found in North America. Their food consists of small fish of all kinds, water insects and vegetable matter. Owing to their comparative rarity they are unlikely to present any problem in a fishery; in fact, they are always a source of great interest to bird-lovers. They all build floating nests among reed beds and care should be taken by any person in a boat not to overrun their nests which they always cover with dead leaves to hide the eggs and to give the nest the appearance of a floating lump of weed.

The kingfisher (*Alcedo ispida*)

This charming little bird is a native of the U K and central and southern Europe. It has allied forms in the U S A, Africa, Asia, and the Far East and Australia. In some countries pollution of rivers and loss of habitat has made it comparatively rare. It takes all kinds of small fish, trout fry included, but unless it finds a pond containing thousands of trout fry or other valuable fish, it can be discounted as a threat to fishing stocks. A severe winter in 1962/63 reduced its European population drastically but its numbers are increasing again. It cannot tackle fish much above 5cm in length and ponds containing many fish of about this length should be netted over.

The wren (*Troglodytes troglodytes*)

This little bird, widely distributed throughout the U S A, South America, the U K and Europe, gets its living by searching for insects in every nook and cranny in obscure, sometimes dark, corners. Hence its name troglodyte. Unfortunately, if it finds its way into hatchery sheds it will eat newly-hatched fry, unless the trays are adequately protected.

Reptiles

Frogs and toads are very harmful to spawn and trout fry and tadpoles compete with fry for food. Although some coarse fish will eat tadpoles, it seems that, according to records, trout rarely do so. The best way to reduce the frog population in a lake is to scoop out the frog spawn and transfer it to some pond where there are no trout, the idea being to conserve the frog population, which is said to be decreasing owing to the destruction of frogs' habitat. Herons will readily eat frogs and thereby relieve the pressure on fisheries to some extent.

Snakes can often be seen swimming near to the margins of lakes during warm weather, probably to clean or cool themselves. They feed mainly on frogs and small rodents, but in some countries will eat small fish.

Invertebrates
As already mentioned, the larvae of water beetles and dragonfly nymphs are voracious feeders on fish fry. In a lake fishery there is no way in which their numbers can be reduced.

Green fish leeches, not very often seen, will attach themselves by their suckers to an adult trout and suck its blood. Thus weakened, the trout becomes easy prey to more leeches and eventually dies of anaemia.

Floods
People may often wonder what happens to fish when a lake or river floods over its banks. It would be natural to suppose that fish would swim over the sides and become stranded or be swept away by the heavy pressure of water. If this happened, fish stocks in rivers would become seriously depleted over the years. In fact, the general evidence is that river fish go down to the bottom and shelter behind reed beds and large stones. Similarly, if a lake floods over its banks, fish go down to the deeper parts and it is extremely unlikely to find a fish stranded when the water level drops. There have been instances, however, after prolonged flooding, with rivers having become indistinguishable from the surrounding fields, where salmon and sea trout have been picked up, but the latter are creatures of passage. Trout, on the other hand, like to stay where they are.

6
Diseases of trout

The owner of a fishery in which the trout are not overcrowded and are virtually in the wild state runs little risk of severe losses due to infectious disease. The only problems are likely to result from pollution of various sorts or lack of oxygen. Nevertheless a working knowledge of the commoner diseases affecting wild fish is necessary, as certain problems may arise from time to time even though the stock of fish introduced were all apparently healthy. The owner will soon learn by observation and experience when it is necessary to seek expert advice.

Diseases of wild trout can be roughly divided into three main groups:

1. Acute infectious disease
2. Diseases manifested by lesions of the skin
3. Mixed group of diseases usually recognized *post mortem.*

Acute infectious diseases
In the wild state acute infectious disease is usually due to bacteria. It is noticed that the fish have not been feeding for a few days when circumstances have been favourable for feeding. Fairly heavy losses start to occur with the appearance of haemorrhagic ulcers on the fish's skin. Even if there are no external lesions, if a dead fish is opened up, it may show patchy haemorrhages of the internal organs, which are the typical signs of acute furunculosis caused by the bacteria *Aeromonas salmonicida.* This infection is more likely to occur with high water temperatures. At lower water temperatures the organism *Corynebacteria* can cause white patchy lesions on the liver, kidney and spleen, with resulting death. Unfortunately these bacteria can sometimes survive in the tissues of the fish and, though the fish does not die it can infect the water.

Less toxic bacteria normally inhabit the skin of fish but, provided the fish is healthy, it suffers no ill-effect; if it dies, the bacteria invade all the body tissues, causing rapid putrefaction.

Hence, when sending a fish for post-mortem it is extremely important that it should be delivered fresh and, if possible, still alive, otherwise it is of no use to the laboratory. The best way to pack them is in moss or fresh leaves in an insulated container; they must not be in water or wrapped in plastic bags. A report should be sent with the fish stating any observations which might be relevant and whether any other fish have died.

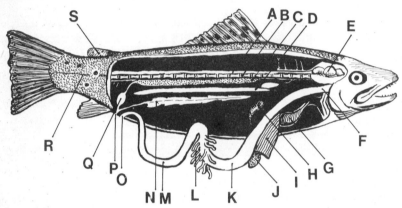

Fig 48 Diagram of anatomy of a trout

A – spinal cord	G – heart	M – intestine
B – vertebral column	H – gall bladder	N – testis or ovary
C – kidney	I – liver	O – anus
D – air bladder	J – spleen	P – urogenital pore
E – brain	K – stomach	Q – urinary bladder
F – gullet	L – pyloric caecae	R – lateral line
		S – adipose fin

Diseases manifested by lesions of the skin

(*a*) As trout become sexually mature around spawning time, certain changes take place in the stomach and intestines and food cannot be digested. In the male the skin becomes thicker and more susceptible to injury which often occurs after fights between male fish in the spawning area. Any wound thus sustained may become infected with the fungal spores of *Saprolegnia*, producing yellowish-white patches round the wound which is soon covered with furry, cotton-wool-like branches of the fungus. If the infection is severe it will rapidly kill the fish, but if mild,

90

the fish should, if possible, be netted out and killed. All fish dying from infectious disease should be buried, preferably in a lime-pit or, failing that, at a good distance from the fishery.

(b) Another disease which is found mainly in mature brown trout is called autumn aeromonad disease which is characterized by inflamed internal organs with blood in the abdominal cavity and sometimes liquefaction of the kidney. There are often patches of fungus on the skin due to *Saprolegnia*. The natural slime which covers a fish's body protects the skin from bacterial invasion and, if this layer is in any way broken by an attack from a predator or by careless handling, infection is likely to follow, either fungal or bacterial or both.

(c) Ulcerative dermal necrosis (UDN) is a disease which many anglers may have seen on salmon and sea trout coming into the rivers of France and the U K in the late sixties. Grey patches first form on the head of the fish and these gradually break down to form red ulcers which become infected with fungus and bacteria. They spread all over the body, eventually killing the fish.

It has not yet been established that brown and rainbow trout can be infected with U D N, but a disease very similar has been found affecting mature fish in the autumn and it is advisable to treat it as though it were infectious and things such as fishing tackle should be disinfected.

(d) There are certain diseases occurring in wild trout which are not related to sexual maturity. These are tumours of the skin, both malignant and benign, and acutely infected skin ulcers. A somewhat raised, bleeding ulcer with rolled edges is typical of a malignant ulcer. A benign tumour is localized and slow-growing, usually without infection or bleeding and may be found only when the fish is gutted. Infections of the skin may take the form of furuncles or boils and are usually caused by *Aeromonas salmonicida*. These appear on the back and sides of older fish and, if they burst, release a highly infectious fluid.

Mixed group of diseases usually discovered *post-mortem*
(a) *Internal parasites*
Many apparently healthy wild trout harbour parasites of one kind or another which, provided the infestation is mild, do not affect their health, but it is often a great disappointment to an angler when opening up a good-sized fish to find the intestine full of worms, and many a good fish has been thrown away because of man's natural revulsion for such creatures.

There are two types of worm dangerous to man if improperly cooked. The first are Anisakis worms, which are small white coiled worms found on the surface of the intestines or liver of sea trout and salmon. The second is the tapeworm *Diphyllobothrium latum*. This has a rather complicated life cycle. The host, often a fish-eating bird, harbours the fully grown tapeworm. The latter releases segments of its body containing eggs which are passed out in faeces into the water. The eggs are eaten by crustaceans such as shrimps or daphnia and these are in turn eaten by a fish. The eggs develop into cysts in the gut wall of the fish and eventually kill it. The dead fish is eaten by a fish-eating bird and so the cycle starts over again. The larger gulls, though they can do a lot of good by removing dead fish from a lake, can be carriers of tapeworms. Brown rats living on the shoreline can also become carriers.

Other more common worms, which are harmless to man, are filariid worms. When a fish is gutted these red worms are seen moving about over the surface of the intestines and present a very unpleasant picture. Usually a large fluid-filled cyst is found in the abdominal cavity to counteract their spread. Round worms are found quite frequently in the intestines but not in great numbers and though they do not greatly affect the fish, they are not very attractive to see.

The worm most harmful to fish if present in large numbers is the thorny-headed worm (*Acanthocephalus*). These are small worms but can be easily seen attached to the mucous membrane of the gut often causing severe haemorrhage and loss of weight. Shrimps can act as an intermediate host for this worm and if introducing shrimps to a newly-made lake, care should be taken that they come from a healthy source.

(b) *External parasites*

The eye fluke (*Diplostomum*) encysts itself in or behind the lens in the eyes of trout, particularly rainbows, causing blindness and eventually death by starvation. In the next stage of the life cycle the fish is eaten by a fish-eating bird in whose faeces the eggs of the parasite are excreted into the water. These are taken up by small snails which after a time release infective cercariae into the water. The latter penetrate the skin of a fish, starting the whole cycle again. Other types of fluke attach themselves to the gills and if heavily infected the fish will die.

The fish louse (*Argulus*), about 5mm long, is sometimes found attached to the skin of a fish but it is of no significance.

The green fish leech, about 3cm long, mentioned in the previous chapter, is easily identified by the suckers at each end of its body through which it draws its victim's blood. It is not a common parasite but a bad infestation might require complete drainage and disinfection of a lake.

The brown leech, commonly found in all fresh water, has one set of suckers on its tail and is completely harmless to trout.

Diseases of nutrition
Fatty degeneration of the liver can be caused by overfeeding with artificial food. Instead of being dark red, the liver is a yellow-brown colour. The remedy is to reduce the food supply. Trout should not be fed when the weather is very hot or when the water temperature is below 6°C.

If a lake is found to contain trout suffering from an infectious disease, there is nothing by way of treatment that can save them. The appropriate authority must be informed and they will give advice about the disposal of the fish and the disinfection of the lake. Quicklime, finely ground up and spread over the lake bottom at the rate of approximately 1,200kg per ha, will kill all parasites, aquatic creatures and all lake weed except that which is very deep rooted. Application of the quicklime must be done during dry weather and with full protective clothing, including goggles; any exposed skin on the face must be covered with Vaseline or similar ointment.

Fortunately, serious infectious disease is rare in trout lakes because all the fish generally come from farms where an extremely close watch is maintained for any sign of a disease that could mean financial ruin to the fish farmer. The fish farmer needs to ensure that the eggs or fingerlings purchased come from healthy stock. With such precautions it is unlikely that serious infectious disease will appear in a fishing lake.

Trout suffering from mild forms of infectious disease have occasionally been caught in rivers and lakes that have never been stocked. Presumably such fish have been infected by the excreta of gulls or other fish-eating birds.

The number of fish affected with parasitic diseases in a properly stocked lake with a good water supply, will be relatively small, and although round worms are commonly found in older fish, young ones are generally free and their rapid turnover in a lake helps to break the life cycle of any parasite they might be harbouring.

Oxygen deficiency

Although this is not a disease in itself, it can quickly lead to a high mortality among trout, which are far more susceptible than carp and other members of the cyprinid group of fishes. It is important, therefore, that whoever is looking after a trout lake should be fully conversant with the symptoms of oxygen deficiency and the rapidity with which it can lead to disaster.

Trout are true natives of the quick-flowing mountain and hill streams where water temperatures seldom exceed 20°C and the presence of many waterfalls maintains the oxygen content at a high level. Trout will also do well in lowland rivers and lakes where there is an abundant supply of good-quality water of sufficient depth to enable them to keep cool in hot weather.

The amount of oxygen held in solution depends on the temperature of the water – the higher the temperature the less oxygen is held. At 0°C the oxygen content in solution is 14.62mg per litre, at 10°C it is 11.33mg per litre, and at 20°C 9.17mg per litre. Trout require not less than 9mg per litre of dissolved oxygen and if the water temperature reaches between 20° and 22°C they begin to show signs of oxygen deficiency; if the temperature rises above 22°C, they will die within a short space of time.

Accurate measurement of water temperature is not easy without a maximum and minimum thermometer because the upper layers of water are warmer than the lower layers, but if the thermometer is lowered to the bottom and then quickly withdrawn, a fairly accurate recording can be made. The best way to reduce the temperature is to increase the flow of water, which is only possible if a sluice can be opened from a main stream, or if water can be pumped from another source.

Another cause of low oxygen content likely to occur in warm, thundery weather, is the decomposition of vegetable matter, a process whereby oxygen is absorbed in large quantities during the night causing a fall below the required level of 9mg per litre; it can also have the undesirable effect of producing excessive oxygen during daylight hours to the point of super-saturation and this too, can endanger the lives of fish.

Trout will die if frozen in ice, but they can survive beneath it provided there is sufficient depth of water and enough oxygen. Plants will keep the water oxygenated if there is a minimum penetration of light through the ice; if light is cut off, however, by a thick covering of snow, an oxygen shortage could develop and trout will perish by asphyxiation. In the event of such a situation arising, it is a wise precaution to sweep the snow away over weed-bearing areas. Usually the feeder stream remains unfrozen and sufficient oxygen is carried in under the ice. Marsh gas may collect beneath the ice, and extend as a broad, silvery sheet; although toxic, it usually escapes from the margins of the ice under the banks before any serious build-up occurs and trout lying in deep water are not likely to be affected.

The first signs of oxygen shortage in fish can be seen when they are swimming on the surface, gulping down air, in much the same way as an unfortunate goldfish is seen swimming in a small bowl of dirty water with its mouth above the surface, trying to get oxygen. At a further stage, when trout become desperate for oxygen, they will leap out of the water, thereby exhausting themselves still further. Some anglers may have mistakenly thought that the fish were rising well, when in fact they were in the final stages of asphyxiation. A trout which has died from oxygen deficiency has a distinctive appearance; the mouth is wide open, the gill covers raised and each gill is widely separated.

If there is a lack of oxygen in the water, emergency measures must be taken. Water can be sprayed into the air over the lake by means of a pump driven from a tractor. If there is a boat available with an outboard engine, this can be used very effectively by passing up and down the lake to churn up the water for as long as possible. A compressor pump, injecting air below the surface of the water, is even better. If it is possible to increase the flow of water into the lake, this should be done.

As a long term measure for lakes in areas where the summers are usually very warm and the water supply not very abundant, it would be advisable to install an aerating machine which can be switched on during any critical period. There are many such machines available and they can be driven by electricity or by a petrol engine. Some of them function on the principle of a fountain where the water is divided into as many droplets as possible, thereby exposing the maximum possible surface to the air for oxygen absorption. Others are made to inject air under pressure from multiple nozzles in a machine placed in a fair depth of water: the greater the depth, the more oxygen is absorbed into the water.

Waterfalls
It is often possible to construct a waterfall in the supply stream to act as a natural oxygenator. This involves making a miniature dam which, of

course, will increase the depth of the supply stream for a considerable distance above the dam and may affect a neighbouring property. This point must be considered before building a waterfall. The construction is relatively simple and can be completed in a day, once the materials are assembled at the site, but there are several very important points to observe.

Two sets of oak boards B (*Figs 49a* and *49b*), of sufficient width to give a height of about 0.5m and long enough to penetrate well into each bank, are fixed vertically to posts driven into the bed of the stream. The distance between the sets of boards should be approximately 1m. It is important to dig the ends of the boards well into the banks otherwise water will find its way round. Pure clay is then packed down tight to fill the space between the boards. More clay is packed against the upstream surface of the boards and sloped down to the bed of the stream.

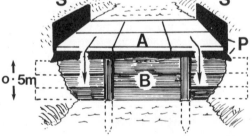

Fig 49a   Side section of waterfall
A – paving stones lying on polythene
B – boarding
P – polythene
S – side board

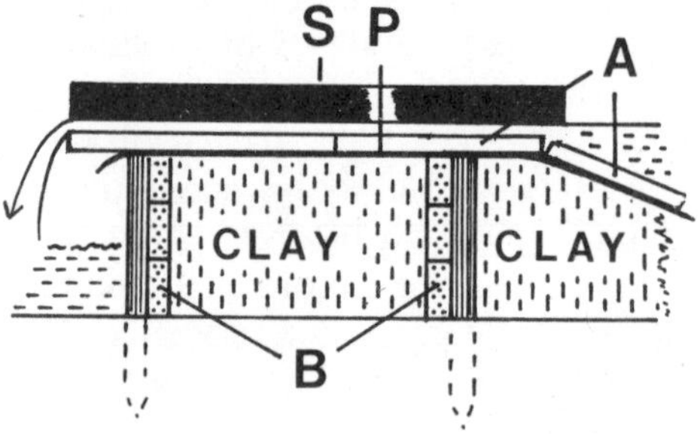

Fig 49b   Front view of small water-
    fall
A – paving stones lying on heavy
    duty polythene
B – boarding extending well into
    banks
P – polythene extending over side
    boards SS'

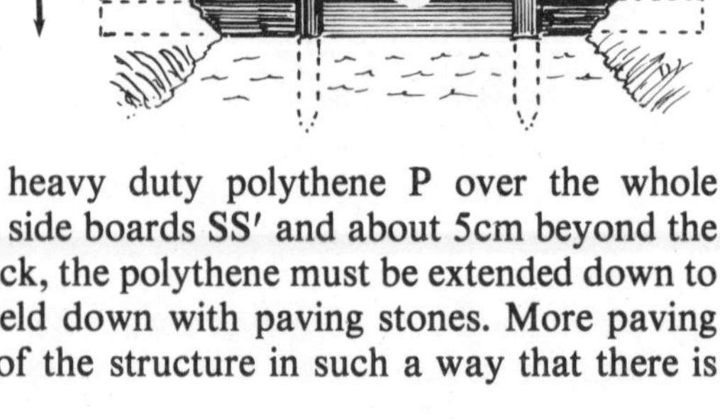

The next step is to lay heavy duty polythene P over the whole structure, extending over the side boards SS' and about 5cm beyond the front set of boards. At the back, the polythene must be extended down to the bed of the stream and held down with paving stones. More paving stones are then laid on top of the structure in such a way that there is sufficient overhang to allow the water to fall freely on the downstream side. The purpose of the polythene is to minimize the erosive action of the water upon the clay and to eliminate the growth of weed. In no way does it act as a waterproofing agent.

This type of waterfall works very well and if properly constructed does not leak or break down. Bags filled with concrete are generally unsatisfactory as water soon finds its way under or around the bags. No amount of plugging with clay will stop the leaks satisfactorily because clay against concrete can never form a complete seal and water soon finds a way between them. This is obviously a job to be carried out when the supply stream is at its lowest, but if there is too much water for easy working, a pump or diversion channel can be used.

Pollution

Polution may occur at any time; it may result from a load of fertilizer falling into a stream, or from a sudden discharge of toxic effluent from a factory or farm. Once pollution has taken place there is nothing to be done about it except to wait until it clears, and this could mean a lapse of two years before a lake or river becomes suitable for trout again. The important thing is to report the damage immediately to the authority responsible for the fisheries in that area and to send off some fish for laboratory examination. If criminal activities are suspected, the police should also be informed.

Detergents can form a very thin layer on the surface of the water and in large quantities can reduce the amount of oxygen that can be absorbed from the atmosphere. They appear as small, white clumps of froth, particularly where the water is turbulent. Careless disposal of waste can easily lead to the poisoning of trout and other fish. In some areas where there are waste heaps from the workings of lead or zinc mines, the metals may get washed out after heavy rains and carried into rivers with serious effects on all aquatic life.

Variations in pH

If the water becomes too acid, *ie* if the pH falls below 5.5 by reason of sudden flooding from peat or conifer-bearing ground, the fish will be affected. A white film appears all over the fish's body and this is an attempt by the skin to neutralize the effect of the acid water by secreting excessive mucus. The gills turn brown and the fish will eventually die, the body remaining in the normal vertical position.

In such a situation, immediate action is required and calcium carbonate should be spread over the water at a rate of about 500kg to the hectare. Where a lake is subject to repeated flooding of this nature, it is advisable to make diversion channels to prevent acid water from entering. The owner should also learn the technique of testing for pH which is done fairly simply by an inexpensive colorimetric apparatus which can usually be purchased at any garden centre. The test consists of mixing a measured amount of water with a measured amount of indicator. The colour of the resulting mixture is then compared with a colour chart which gives the appropriate pH value.

Much has been heard recently about the serious effect of sulphur dioxide in the atmosphere falling as acid rain in certain parts of the Northern Hemisphere particularly in Canada, Scandinavia and northern Europe and causing very serious loss of life among fish and other aquatic creatures. It would seem that these countries have very good reason to be alarmed. In very dry weather, trees and other vegetation act as a depository for sulphur dioxide which, when it rains heavily, is converted chemically into an acid and, if this is washed into a lake, a dramatic drop in pH may occur, even to as low as 4.5, a level at which no fish will survive. Sulphur dioxide also leaches out gradually the elements in the soil which are essential to plant life and many conifers in the forests of northern Europe are becoming stunted or are dying. If the water becomes too alkaline, that is above pH 9.0, fish will suffer from burns of the skin. Such an occurrence is unlikely in a well-managed lake with water of a pH just above 7, when it is most stable, but it might occur as the result of pollution or after the use of quicklime.

To summarize, it is most improbable that infectious diseases will appear in trout lakes when normal precautions against overcrowding are taken and where the water is of good quality. There is always a faint risk that disease may be introduced by gulls or waterfowl but this risk is very small because those responsible for the movement of fish are quick to eradicate any known source of disease and prohibit all movement of fish in the infected area.

Oxygen deficiency in trout, however, is something for which the owner of a fishery must be always on the alert, particularly in very hot weather, or if the lake is covered with ice. Weed must be carefully controlled to reduce the chance of a build-up of nitrogenous products.

7
Lake environment

Anyone who decides to build a lake must realize that a permanent alteration to the surrounding countryside will arise and therefore every effort must be made to ensure that when the lake is finished it should merge, as far as possible, with the landscape. There will be severe criticism and comments by the local inhabitants if its appearance offends them. The shape of the lake, as already mentioned, should be irregular, conforming as far as it is feasible with the natural lie of the land.

A lake is there to be seen. All the great landscape designers of the eighteenth century made it the central feature of an estate and it was constructed in such a way that a view of it could be obtained from all the main rooms of the house. The modern lake builder should try to follow this principle, and though time to enjoy the view may be limited it will be easier to monitor the lake and its surroundings. During heavy thaws or after cloudbursts unexpected things can happen. An outflow pipe may get blocked by excessive debris and cause a sudden rise in water levels, or the level may drop for some reason.

Trees
The correct disposition of trees round a trout lake is of great importance. If there are too many big trees overhanging the lake margins, not enough sunlight will penetrate the water and, without sunlight, photosynthesis cannot take place. This is a vital process by which aquatic plants absorb carbon dioxide from the water and convert it into carbohydrate to make plant growth, and the plants release oxygen into the water during the day.

Another reason is that there is very little movement of air over water sheltered by trees. When the surface of a stretch of water is agitated by wind, a considerable amount of oxygen is absorbed which may be important to the survival of the trout during hot weather. That this is no theory was clearly established when, in a certain very sheltered lake during the summer of 1976, many trout were found dead from lack of oxygen, whereas in a lake only a mile away, exposed to all available breeze, there were no casualties.

Another and obvious reason for not having trees overhanging a lake is that fishing is made extremely difficult. There is nothing more frustrating and embarrassing for anglers than to spend much fishing time disentangling their lines from surrounding tree branches (see *Fig 50*). Too many overhanging trees will result in debris falling into the water during spring and autumn. When severe gales occur large branches – if not the tree itself – may be blown into the water, possibly causing obstruction to outflow systems. The removal of a fallen tree from a lake is a major operation and extremely expensive, but it must be removed, otherwise fishing is likely to be impaired and lines broken.

It is not suggested that existing trees standing well away from the lake should be removed, but only large overhanging trees or any tree whose roots might spread into the dam or overflow system. This should be done when the lake is being built and the necessary machinery is on the site; it will be well worth the expense.

Fig 50   A good trout lake but too many trees on one side

It is a good plan, however, to plant a few alder trees (*Alnus glutinosa*) on the bank in such a position that they provide shade for trout and therefore cooler water. In very hot weather, fish will normally go down to the bottom of the lake to seek the cooler water; if some shade is provided, however, they may continue feeding on the surface, to the angler's advantage. Alders are a natural river-side tree. They are easy to transplant and should be kept short and bushy by annual clipping of the leading shoots. Their broad leaves afford protection for insect life of various kinds, many of which drop into the water to become food for trout. The roots of these trees furnish the trout with very good 'lies', a fact that any angler will soon discover.

Willow palm (*Salix caprea*) and weeping willow (*Salix tristis*) are not nearly so useful as providers of shade as the alder, and, unless they are cut back annually, will get out of hand. Crack willow (*Salix fragilis*) is one to avoid. As its Latin name suggests, it has very brittle branches, both big and small, and in high winds these will drop off in large numbers. If a branch drops off and sticks into the ground it will readily take root. Most of the pollarded willows, so commonly seen, are crack willows and were planted to prevent bank erosion which, with their huge root system, they do very effectively. Most types of willow produce salicylic acid, the basis of aspirin, and large quantities of willow leaves falling into a pond may produce toxic conditions for fish. Where there is running water, this would not apply. It is said that Napoleon's soldiers, on their retreat from Moscow, found that by chewing willow bark they obtained some relief from their pain and misery.

If a lake is exposed to the wind, fishing can sometimes be very difficult and, in the early months of the season, extremely cold. A belt of the quick-growing *Cupressus leylandii* or *C lawsonii*, set well back from the lake, is probably the best answer; these trees can be topped and will bush out well, and make a good wind break. Sitka spruce (*Picea sitchensis*) is quick-growing and will thrive in wet conditions but responds badly to pruning and the lower branches die off, giving less protection from the wind.

The provision of several small inlets with corresponding promontories will greatly improve the appearance of the lakeside and make it more pleasant for fishing. Few anglers want to form part of a long line of fishermen. A few small, bushy alder trees, strategically planted, will be very helpful in creating a little privacy for the anglers who like a quiet corner to themselves.

For those wishing to attract wildfowl, it is essential to keep the lake-sides open and clear of big trees. All wild duck are extremely cautious and well they might be. Before coming in to settle on a stretch of water, they will always circle round several times and be on the lookout for any suspicious object that might give them cause for concern. Once they are satisfied that all is safe, they fly in up-wind to land on to the most open part of the lake; even then they are very nervous and remain for some time in a state of readiness for an instant take-off. If there is too much cover, wild duck will view it with mistrust and move on elsewhere; the only time they appreciate thick cover is during the breeding season.

Fishing hut
The obvious place to erect a hut is under the protection of a windbreak. The usefulness of such a shelter far outweighs its cost. Much of the equipment anglers always carry can be stored in it, as well as tools, ropes, oars, trout food and, perhaps most important of all, it provides somewhere to sit and take refreshment in comparative comfort during inclement weather. If a window is installed, this should be carefully boarded up when the hut is not in use in order to deter any vandals from trying to effect a break-in.

Lake-side vegetation
A lake without a fringe of reeds round its shoreline looks bare and uninteresting, but apart from general appearance there are two good reasons why it should have a fringe of well-controlled vegetation round its margins.

The first is that insect life flourishes on the half-submerged plants and lake flies, of all sorts, lay their eggs on the stems. Their nymphs and larvae, when ready to hatch into their adult forms, crawl up the stems and undergo their metamorphoses in a protected area, away from wind and concealed from their natural enemies.

The second reason is that anglers like a fringe of vegetation between themselves and the water to give some concealment from the sharp eyes of the trout. If there is no such screen, an angler walking along the bank will temporarily scare away all the fish in that area. The wise angler makes full use of a screen of vegetation to hide as much of his body as possible, both when fishing and when moving up and down the lake-side.

Trout have very acute vision. They have a mobile spherical lens in each eye giving them very good all-round underwater vision and there is no doubt they can distinguish colours. They also have light-sensitive cells in their retinae which enable them to change their body colour to suit their environment. Their vision of things above the surface of the water is much more limited due to the refraction or bending of the light rays entering the water. They see the sky as if through a large circular window; beyond the edges of this circle, they can see only the mirror-like, undersurface of the water. A fly landing on the surface of the water within the circular window would be seen in full detail but if it lands outside the circle, only that part of the body below the mirror surface would be visible to a trout. If there is a slight ripple on the water, a trout's vision of the outside world is very much distorted and the angler's line floating on the water is less easily seen. Such conditions are ideal for trout fishing.

Despite this theoretical limitation of vision, in practice a trout seems to be able to see anyone within 25m all too easily if there is no reed cover. If only the head and shoulders of the angler are visible, the rest of the body being concealed by vegetation, a trout is less likely to be scared away.

At this point it is as well to mention the hearing capacity of trout. Like other vertebrates, fish have an internal ear, the labyrinth, which is the organ of hearing, balance and orientation. Hearing ability varies very much from one type of fish to another. The carp family have a well-developed sense of hearing and minnows even better. In addition fish have a 'lateral line', a sensitive nerve which runs down the sides of the body with nerve branches over the head. This acts like radar, giving the fish a picture of objects around it, including other fish, and it will easily pick up vibration waves made by an angler's heavy tread along a bank. It has been established that blind fish can survive quite well for some time because of the sensitivity of the lateral line.

To provide the sort of concealment the angler requires, it is best to plant the common sedge (*Cladium mariscus*). Of all the marginal aquatic plants, it is the easiest to control by cutting and consequently there is no difficulty in clearing small gaps along the shoreline where anglers can land their fish. It has a natural tendency to spread its roots into the lake, but less vigorously than some other reed families.

The common reed (*Phragmites australis*) known in the U K as Norfolk reed and used for thatching, is not recommended for lakeside cover because it has a massive root system which spreads into the lake and is difficult to control.

The common rush (*Eleocharis palustris*), with its spikey, rounded leaves, growing everywhere on bog land, does not offer nearly as much cover, but it has two advantages: first, it is tough and deep-rooted, forming an excellent defence against bank erosion; secondly, being a plant that does not like its roots completely submerged, it will not spread into the lake to any extent but has a tendency to range itself along the shoreline (*Fig 51*).

A warning must be given concerning the planting of yellow flag iris (*Iris pseudacorus*) and branched bur-reed (*Sparganium erectum*). They spread by sending out large creeping roots into the lake and, if left undisturbed, will collect silt and debris, eventually converting a large part of the lake into a bog. The roots produce shoots that may suddenly appear 3 or 4m distant from the original plant; these shoots must be grubbed up before the roots become permanent.

Also the greater reedmace (*Typha latifolia*), often wrongly named 'bulrush', and the lesser reedmace (*Typha augustifolia*) are not recomended for fishing lakes. The former can grow up to 2m tall and would present a hazard to the angler's line. The brown heads of these plants contain many thousands of seeds which are scattered far and

Fig 51 The common rush (*Eleocharis palustris*) planted round an island to prevent wave erosion

wide by the wind and easily propagate themselves so that they are liable to appear spontaneously on a lake-side. They grow out from the shoreline and it is better to pull them out before they spread. During the autumn, when the foliage dies back, they become an untidy mass of stalks and leaves.

Edible watercress (*Nasturtium officinale*) is extremely useful for aquatic animals, particularly shrimps and snails, and will grow well from cuttings held down by stones.

Marsh marigolds (*Caltha palustris*) will root quite easily on the lake margins and are delightful to see in the early spring and they continue flowering for two months, their foliage giving excellent cover for aquatic flies.

Other attractive wild flowers are the great willow herb (*Epilobium hirsutum*), meadowsweet (*Filipendula ulmaria*), which used to be strewn on the floors in the 16th century to cut down unsavoury smells, and the common foxglove (*Digitalis purpurea*). Such flowers will greatly improve the appearance of the lakeside and can easily be cut back if they interfere too much with casting.

Behind the lake-side vegetation, it is advisable to make a level footpath free from tufts of grass or holes in the ground. It is much easier to walk quietly on level ground. An angler walking along the bank is usually watching the water for rising trout and often does not look where he is going. If he trips over a tuft of grass it may possibly amuse some of his fellow anglers, but it will certainly scare away the fish in the vicinity and he may injure himself or break his rod.

Lake weeds

Most authorities agree that it is unnecessary to introduce weed into a new lake because many types of waterweed will eventually appear by themselves. On no account should Canadian pondweed (*Elodea canadensis*) (*Fig 52*), a plant introduced from North America, be put in, even though it is one of the best oxygenators of all. If a bucketful of this weed is thrown into a lake with a muddy bottom as opposed to a stoney one, within two years it will have spread and taken root in all but the deepest parts; if allowed to grow freely, it will eventualy choke the lake altogether. Should the water supply to the lake come from a source where there is Canadian pondweed, it is advisable to erect a filter system to prevent the weed from getting through. It is a plant that multiplies by budding and only rarely by seed and is unlikely, therefore, to appear spontaneously unless carried in by a bird.

Fig 52   Canadian pondweed
(*Elodea canadensis*)

Other underwater plants such as: water milfoil (*Myriophyllum spicatum*), water starwort (*Callitriche stagnalis*), water violet (*Hottonia palustris*), water crowfoot (*Ranunculus aquatalis*), will probably appear spontaneously within a year or two in a new lake, their spores being brought in by the wind or on the feet or in the excreta of waterfowl. These plants are less efficient than Canadian pondweed as oxygenators but they do not have the ferocious rate of growth of the latter and are therefore quite welcome.

Plants with floating leaves with their roots in the bottom, such as the white water lily (*Nymphaea alba*) and the yellow water lily (*Nuphar lutea*) can be put in. These are quite useful in a lake provided they can be kept localized to a small area, because they provide welcome shade and very good feeding grounds for trout, but their long leaf-stems can be a particular hazard for the angler's line if a fish is hooked.

Frog-bit (*Hydrocharis morsus-ranae*) with its heartshaped leaves and small white flowers and water soldier (*Stratiotes aloides*), also with white flowers, are both common and make prolific growth by producing long runners and they will soon form a solid mass of weed unless kept under control.

There are several types of duckweed which float freely with their roots hanging down in the water. They occur most frequently on still water which has a high organic content such as in ponds where cattle have been standing, and are unlikely to be found on lakes except in very sheltered corners.

Algae appear spontaneously and form a huge group of plants with varying complexity of structure, some having single cells, others groups of cells and their classification is very complicated. They may be coloured red, brown, blue-green, yellow-green or green, but they all contain chlorophyll and function like higher water plants, taking in carbon dioxide and giving off oxygen.

The very common dark brown algae, which at first sight look rather like sewage, bob up from the lake bottom in little clumps and lie on the surface to collect in great masses, making fishing almost impossible unless there is a sufficient breeze to blow them to the shoreline. The not so common red algae can cause a lake to turn a red-brown colour and may create considerable alarm amongst those who do not know the reason; no doubt this phenomenon has been the source of much superstition in the past. The most troublesome are the green, threadlike, filamentous algae, known as 'blanket weed'. These algae can obstruct outflow systems but fortunately they can easily be netted out, unlike the other kinds of algae which break up on contact. A cool spell of weather in the summer slows down their growth but as soon as the sun comes out, they start to appear again. Most algae start to disappear late in August as the nights get cooler and the water temperature drops.

All the above plants, including algae, play a very important part in the ecology of a lake and without them the small aquatic creatures could not survive. Anyone who pulls out a lump of weed from a freshwater lake will see that it usually contains many shrimps, snails, nymphs and other small aquatic animals which are all the natural food of the trout. But there can be too much weed; if a fishing water becomes choked the fish cannot move about freely to feed and will eventually get caught up in it and die. There is also the very real danger that the decomposition of excessive weed will create a shortage of oxygen in the water by its conversion to carbon dioxide. If there is too little weed, as is often the case in lakes with rocky bottoms in hilly disticts, the fish find less food and their rate of growth is slower. The aim therefore is to maintain a moderate growth of aquatic weed.

Weed control

The removal of excess weed from a lake is one of the least pleasant and most time-consuming tasks a lake owner may have to carry out. If there is a good deal of shallow water round the sides of the lake and the bottom is firm, the old-fashioned scythe is the best instrument to use. Some sort of tool, such as a fork bent out at right angles, should be employed for grubbing up spreading roots. Weed in deeper water, out of reach of a scythe, calls for a hand weed-cutting appliance (*Fig 53*). It needs two people to work the cutter and a third person to row the boat. The cutter consists of a series of steel blades with sharp serrated edges, all linked together end-to-end, each blade being twisted in such a way that a cutting edge is always presented to the weed stems. A chain is attached to each end of the set of cutter blades to weigh them down in the water and to the end of each chain a rope is attached. With one person on the bank and another in the boat, the cutter is worked slowly forwards under the weed with a sawing action. The weed comes rapidly to the surface. It is advisable to cut over the area several times, otherwise patches are missed.

Removal of cut weed is essential. If it is not taken away, especially Canadian pondweed, some of it will regenerate elsewhere in the lake and the rest will form rotting debris on the bottom, reducing the oxygen content of the water. Fortunately there is usually a breeze on an open

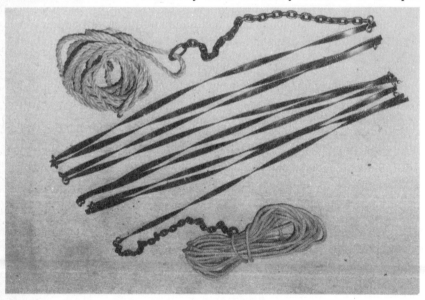

Fig 53   Weed-cutting gear

108

lake, sufficient to blow most of the cut weed to one bank or another from where it can be forked out on to dry land. On very large lakes mechanical weed-cutters are used, operated from a special boat with paddles at the stern, but for smaller lakes the cost of such a machine would be prohibitive.

In the U S A shoreline weeds in small lakes and ponds are got rid of by a 'draindown' or a lowering of the water level until the weeds are fully exposed and can be raked out. If there are fish in the water, the level must be lowered only enough to expose the shoreline weed. The water is pumped or siphoned out. It is important to choose cool, cloudy weather for this job, otherwise the fish may suffer.

Biological methods of weed control

Experiments are now being carried out with grass carp (*Ctenopharyngodon idella*) to find a natural way of controlling excessive weed. This species of carp which has long been cultivated in the Far East as a food fish, is entirely herbivorous and will feed off most of the common aquatic plants, including Canadian pondweed. However, it is not altogether acclimatized to the temperatures of the Northern Hemisphere but it would seem that, when these fish are freely available, it might be a great advantage to have a limited number in a trout lake to control the weed in countries where the winters are very mild. They would not compete for food with the trout and would be unlikely to breed as the conditions in the average lake would be unfavourable.

Swans feed almost exclusively on water weed. A pair of swans and their brood of cygnets will consume vast quantities of underwater weed and reed shoots at the height of summer when growth of weed is most troublesome to the anglers. Nearly all ducks make up a large part of their diet from vegetable matter and they are very fond of the shoots of submerged waterweed, including Canadian pondweed. With their comparatively short necks they control the surface weed down to a depth of about 40cm, leaving adequate cover for aquatic animals in the weed they cannot reach. Thus they clear the surface weed which is most troublesome to the angler's line.

In the author's experience on a millstream, about a dozen mallard kept the weed under very good control over 150 yards of stream. Before the duck were introduced, it was necessary to clear out the weed twice during the summer, a very tiresome and expensive operation. After the ducks were introduced no such clearing was necessary, and much less mud was deposited on the bottom due to the improved rate of flow of water. The mallard are hand-reared, and may be free-flying or pinioned, but they must be fed regularly on corn, which would seem to be a justifiable expense if they control the weed. Too many ducks on a lake or on water which is not free-flowing will foul the water, but a limited number are beneficial by fertilizing the lake bottom and creating food for algae and other small aquatic creatures, so starting the food chain.

Canada geese (*Branta canadensis*) are natives of North America migrating south during the winter often as far as the Gulf of Mexico. They were introduced to the U K some two centuries ago where they have become well established. They do not eat much waterweed but crop the grass round the lake-side. Like all geese they are always on the watch for predators and, though they do not give an audible alarm call, it is often possible to see from a distance if they have been disturbed. As already mentioned they will drive off herons.

Chemical control of weed

It is generally accepted that herbicides have no direct toxic effect on fish and aquatic animals, but they have not been in use long enough to establish whether there is any harmful long-term effect from their frequent application.

The use of chemicals is very much limited by the fact that many lakes have their inflow and outflow on a main watercourse but if it is possible to cut off the inflow temporarily, thus preventing the chemically treated water from entering the mainstream, the use of chemicals would probably be permitted by a Water Authority. For example, if water is abstracted from a river to form a lake (*Fig 4*) and returned to the river lower downstream, it would be quite easy to shut off the water for four or five days during which time the chemical herbicide would have become inactive; it would also be possible to use a herbicide if the outflow from a lake had stopped due to drought.

One of the main risks in the use of herbicides is not their toxicity to fish but that the decomposition of weed on the lake bottom may cause a considerable lowering of oxygen content in the water. To reduce the likelihood of this happening, the operation should always be carried out in dull and preferably cool weather when the oxygen content of the water is higher. If the weed is very thick, only a small part of the lake should be treated at a time.

Herbicides are effective only in standing or sluggish water. They will

110

kill Canadian pondweed, water crowfoot, water milfoil, duckweed and frog-bit. Sedges, reeds and bur-reed are slightly affected. Methods have not yet been devised of keeping the concentration in running water sufficiently high to kill weeds. Herbicides must, of course, be handled very carefully and gloves, Wellingtons and protective clothing should be worn. It is difficult to assess the correct quantity to use where the depth of water is not precisely known and the manufacturer's instructions should be followed exactly to avoid an 'overdose'.

It would seem, therefore, that in the present state of our knowledge, the use of herbicides would be justified only where weed had reached such proportions as to make a lake uninhabitable for fish; this is what happened in the author's lake (see frontispiece). At the end of May, large masses of Canadian pondweed started to appear all round the shallower parts of the lake. If this had been left to grow, it would have choked all except the deepest parts within a matter of weeks. Manual cutting was tried but proved to be inadequate. As the water level of the lake had dropped considerably and there was no outflow, it was decided to use a proprietary product containing Diquat, the weather being dull and cool at the time and ideal for spraying.

The operation is quite simple to carry out. Using a plastic pressure sprayer with a long nozzle, the correct amount of herbicide is measured out and put into the sprayer which is then topped up with water and the pressure pumped up. Sitting in a boat, which must be rowed slowly, the operator keeps the nozzle of the sprayer well below the surface and sprays into the weed.

The lake in question had an area of about 0.9ha and a cubic capacity of 17,000m^3. The amount of herbicide used was 15 litres and only one third of the lake was treated, as a precaution against killing off too much weed. At the end of a week the Canadian pondweed in the area sprayed had all disappeared and was starting to die in the untreated area. Some of the reeds which had spread into the water were beginning to wilt. The colour of the water changed very slightly to a brownish tinge but not a single dead trout in a stock of about 150 was found during the months following nor was there any visible effect on the small aquatic life in the lake, the shrimps being as numerous and active as ever. Unfortunately it was not possible to see how much regeneration of weed occurred in the years following, as the property passed into other hands, but it would probably be optimistic to think that further applications of herbicide would be unnecessary.

Lake islands

An island in a lake always improves its general appearance. It will be beneficial to the fish because extra feeding grounds in the shallower water round the island are provided; it will also offer extra trout lies where fish will be less harassed by the angler's line and will be able to attain a really good size and thus present a challenge to the more expert angler.

Planting a small island with large trees is very inadvisable as leaves and branches will fall in the water. At most a few evergreen shrubs such as rhododendrons (*Rhododendron ponticum*) should be planted if the soil is suitable, or better still some weed-excluding plant such as rose of Sharon (*Hypericum*) or one of the colourful *Ajuga* plants with their mat-forming habit of growth. Heather or bracken could also be used. Marsh marigolds planted on the water's edge will provide excellent cover for aquatic flies and some shelter for trout.

The banks of an island are very exposed to the erosive effect of wave action. To prevent this happening it is wise to plant a few roots of the common, spikey rush which will spread itself conveniently round the water line and form a tough barrier against erosion (*Fig 51*). Such an island will very likely be chosen as a nesting site by a pair of swans or Canada geese. It is better to have swans nesting in the middle of a lake rather than on a bank where the cob swan can make himself extremely unpleasant to an angler.

Finally, it is essential to erect a fence all round the lake and make it proof against sheep and cattle. It should be placed far enough away from the lake so as not to create problems for anglers when casting. If cattle can get to a lake, they will soon ruin the banks and foul the water; if the bottom is sticky clay, they may get stuck and eventually drown themselves. Cattle are inquisitive creatures and any angler who has tried fishing where there is a herd of cows trampling round his equipment and lunch basket, will soon realize that the cost of a fence is fully justified. Sheep are rather less of a nuisance and take good care not to get their feet wet, but in large numbers they will nibble down too much of the vegetation round the margins and foul the grass. If the grass is very thick, it might be sensible to have a few sheep to keep the grass short.

An unfenced lake is an open invitation to hikers and picknickers, but a good stout fence will go some way to solving the problem, plus a prominent notice indicating that the property is private and fishing prohibited. A quickthorn hedge, planted inside the fence so that it cannot

112

be eaten by cattle, might be well worth consideration. As the fence deteriorates and posts begin to rot, the thorn hedge should be high enough to keep intruders away and eventually furnish a formidable barrier, which will have a more pleasing appearance than barbed wire. *Rosa rugosa* is also inexpensive and rapidly grows into a fine prickly barrier.

A gate is essential to allow the lorry transporting new fish stocks to get as near as possible to the lake-side. It will also be needed for tractors and possibly other heavy machinery.

The reader may be inclined to think that too much emphasis has been placed on improving the lake surroundings and that the expense would not be justifiable. It is certainly true that many of the suggestions made above could involve a considerable financial outlay but in the long run a well-stocked lake, set in pleasant surroundings with a good degree of angler comfort, is more than likely to pay for itself.

8
Coarse fishing and other uses

If a lake owner decides to stock coarse fish instead of trout, it could be a very wise decision, especially if the lake is in the vicinity of a large town. Coarse fishing has always been a popular sport. In recent years more and more people have taken to it and, like many other sports, it has become highly competitive and offers considerable financial rewards to the more skilful. Anglers are always looking for new fishing waters and are very willing to pay well for the right to fish.

The ideal lake for coarse fishing is one which lies not much above sea level where the water temperature will be considerably warmer than, for example, in a lake 500m or more above sea level. Coarse fish thrive better where there is plenty of silt and good weed growth and they are less sensitive to oxygen deficiency than trout.

Stocking a lake with coarse fish is very different from stocking with trout only. In the latter case, the owner always knows more or less how many trout there are in the lake by deducting the number caught from the number stocked and allowing a percentage for natural wastage, but in coarse fishing, where the catch is usually returned to the water, it is difficult after two or three seasons to estimate the relative numbers of each type of fish because some of them, such as perch and roach, breed more quickly than others.

Most coarse fish lay several hundred thousand eggs during each breeding season, the eggs being attached to weed, sticks and other objects lying on the bottom. They start laying as soon as the temperature of the water begins to rise in April and May. The survival rate for coarse fish spawn is very low. It is eagerly eaten by other fish, frogs and aquatic creatures like dragonfly nymphs, as well as ducks, moorhens, coots and water shrews. On average, eggs hatch within about one week; the warmer the water the quicker they hatch. The newly-

114

hatched fry are immediately subject to attack by the same above-mentioned predators, so the number of fish reaching maturity is usually not more than one or two per cent; however, some coarse fish seem to breed more successfully than others, thereby leading to the over-population of one species to the detriment of another and a general slowing down in growth rate because of strong competition for the available food.

The following are species of coarse fish most popular with anglers and suitable for stocking in low-lying lakes in countries where the climate is not subject to extremes of heat and cold.

Carp (*Cyprinus carpio*)

Originating in Asia, the carp was brought into Europe 2,000 years ago and has been cultivated as a food-fish ever since and survives well in countries below latitude 60°N. In the U S A it has thrived so well that it is regarded as somewhat of a nuisance to the angler because it makes the stream muddy with its foraging and it has been banned in all but 19 states. It is now of great commercial importance in France, Germany, Poland, Czechoslovakia, Austria, Yuogslavia, Hungary and the U S S R and the total commercial catch is estimated to be 200,000 tonnes annually. It is sold commercially at a weight of about 1kg. In the wild state, under favourable conditions, it can attain a weight of 30kg and live up to 40 years.

Carp is a very popular fish with some anglers as it is cunning and difficult to catch and, if hooked, will put up a good fight. It is therefore quite an angling achievement to land a 15kg fish.

Wild carp seldom breed successfully unless the water temperature in May and June reaches 17–20°C. It must not be confused with the crucian carp (*Carassius carassius*) which is smaller but extremely hardy and can resist pollution, oxygen deficiency and low temperatures more easily than other freshwater fishes. It is stocked sometimes in ponds where the common carp cannot survive but it is unwise to introduce crucian carp into ponds where there are the more valuable common carp, as not only will they compete for food but they act as a reservoir for carp parasites.

Common bream (*Abramis brama*)

The bream is common in slow-flowing rivers and in lakes where the bottom is muddy. It is sometimes found in brackish water. Its range extends from the U K as far as the Caspian sea. In Europe it is popular as a food-fish and is usually caught with stake-nets. A mature fish can grow to an average weight of 2kg and is a good fish for angling.

The tench (*Tinca tinca*)
The tench is a very suitable fish for stocking in a lake with a muddy bottom and good weed growth. It can survive oxygen deficiency better even than carp but, like the latter, can only spawn successfully in the wild if the water temperature in May is about 19–20°C. It is a popular fish with anglers and, being a bottom feeder, can be caught with worms or aquatic insects. In Europe and particularly Germany, its flesh is regarded as a delicacy and fetches a good price. A mature fish on average weighs about 2kg.

Perch (*Perca fluviatilis*)
The perch is widely distributed over Europe and northern parts of Asia. There are many species, the American yellow perch (*P fluviatilis flavescens*) being found in the eastern parts of North America. The perch is a good angling fish and can be caught with fly, spinner or with worms or small fish. It rarely attains much weight, an eight-year-old fish, 25cm long, will weigh about 0.2kg.

They are successful breeders and a lake is liable to become over-populated by them, resulting in a general reduction in growth rate through lack of food. Perch feed on most aquatic animals and as they get older will eat small roach and other fish including young perch.

Zander or pike-perch (*Stizostedion lucioperca*)
Zander originates from Europe, parts of Scandinavia and western Asia. It has been introduced into some eastern counties of the U K where it has thrived but measures to stop further introductions have been taken. It is an excellent game fish. When five to six years old it will weigh about 1kg but as it matures its weight can increase to a maximum of about 12kg. Like pike, it feeds entirely on small fish and may be taken on a spinner. In the countries of its origin it is considered good to eat and about 10,000 tonnes are taken annually.

Sun perches (Centrarchidae)
The large-mouth black bass (*Micropterus salmoides*) and the small-mouth black bass (*Micropterus dolomieu*) originate in North America.

116

They have been introduced to Europe where they do not thrive very well. In the U S A it is regarded as an excellent angling fish and bass weighing up to 10kg are sometimes caught. Black bass are extremely voracious fish and for this reason the 'bluegill sunfish' (*Leopomis machrochirus*), a vegetarian and a very rapid breeder, is put in for the bass to feed on. In Europe bass are sometimes used to keep down valueless fish in deep ponds.

Roach (*Rutilus rutilus*)

The roach is widely distributed throughout the U K, Europe, Scandinavia, central and eastern Asia. It is a common fish in lakes and slow-flowing streams and is quite tolerant of minor degrees of pollution. It is a very successful breeder and its young provide the natural food for larger fish such as pike, zander and perch. It is of no great value as a food-fish, except in eastern Europe but in Europe and the U K it is regarded as a most important fish for angling. It rarely reaches much more than 10–15cm in length except in very favourable conditions when it may reach 25cm and 1kg in weight.

Rudd (*Scardinius erythrophthalmus*)

Rudd is a natural inhabitant of lakes and is widely distributed from the U K and Europe to eastern Asia. It breeds freely and is regarded by anglers as good sporting fish, though averaging only 10–20cm in length.

Dace (*Leuciscus leuciscus*)

Dace has the same distribution as the rudd, but is found only in clear-flowing streams.

Pike (*Esox lucius*)

Pike is found in North America, Canada, the U K, Europe and the temperate zones of Asia. It inhabits well-weeded waters in lakes and rivers and is renowned as an excellent game-fish. It can reach a weight of 8–10kg at the age of about 12 years and can present a real challenge to the angler. The catch of a European pike over 30 years old and weighing 35kg has been recorded. In some European countries it is not only regarded as an excellent game-fish but also as very good to eat when weighing around 5kg. About 10,000 tonnes are eaten every year.

The pike's growth rate compared with other fish is fast. From a very early age, when only 4cm long, the young pike begins to prey on the fry of bream, roach, perch and others – and it remains piscivorous through its life, even consuming smaller pike. For this reason, when stocking a lake with pike it must be remembered that unless all the fish are of the same size, the bigger ones will eat the smaller ones. The same principle applies when a lake is being netted out; all the large pike must be removed, unless they are to be left to eat the smaller ones and grow bigger still. Pike are particular about the size of the prey they consume. A large pike about 70cm long prefers to eat medium-sized trout 25cm long, in fact just about the size of trout which are sold for stocking a lake. It will prey on the smaller trout only when it cannot find the size it likes best. The popular theory that pike will clean up the small and weak fish first is not a valid one.

Pike are sometimes introduced deliberately for a certain period into ponds which contain a lot of unwanted small roach or crucian carp. They are also stocked into large lakes where the roach population has got out of hand.

Eel (*Anguilla anguilla*)
Eels can be found in most rivers and lakes in Europe, Eire, the U K, Scandinavia and in Mediterranean countries. An eel, truly a sea fish, spends about 10 years of its fascinating life cycle in fresh water where it feeds on larvae, snails, crustaceans and small fish and is said to eat the spawn of trout and other fish.

From an angler's point of view, it is of little value and competes for food with more useful fish, but in Europe and the Far East, especially Japan, it is highly rated as a food delicacy and there is always a ready market for elvers which are grown on to a marketable size in eel farms.

It is impossible to find out the number of eels in a fishery because they are rarely caught by anglers, being nocturnal feeders, but if a lake is emptied for any reason, the owner will doubtless be very surprised at the number of eels of all sizes present.

To reduce the eel population a trap can be set. This consists of a wire cage of 1cm mesh with two compartments; a wire funnel leads from the outside into the first compartment and a second wire funnel leads into the second compartment which is baited with pieces of fish or a bunch of worms. At the end of the trap a wire door is fixed for baiting and removal of the catch. The trap should be about 0.75m long and the funnel openings 4cm in diameter. It is an efficient trap and will catch half-grown and fully-grown eels if set during the warmer months of the year when they are feeding most actively.

Catfish (Ictaluridae)
Of North American origin, the catfish has been introduced to France and central Europe. It lives in the mud at the bottom of lakes and slow-moving rivers and feeds on aquatic animals and small fish. Although it will take a hook, it is not regarded as a good fish for angling. The flesh is yellow and rather sweet in flavour. It should be skinned before cooking. The maximum weight is about 2kg.

Stickleback, bleak and swamp-minnow
A brief mention must be made of the smaller fish which inhabit lakes, such as the stickleback (*Gasterosteus aculeatus*), the pond loach (*Misgurnus fossilis*), the bleak (*Alburnus alburnus*) and the swamp-minnow (*Phoxinus percnurus*). None of these are of any use in an angling water and they compete for food with more valuable fish and should not therefore be deliberately introduced.

Management of a coarse fishery
Coarse fish anglers may be divided roughly into three groups.

The first group are those who go fishing for a pleasant outing, perhaps with some of the family, with no definite object in view, the size and type of the catch being of no importance.

The second group is usually made up of experienced anglers who have become specialists in catching one particular type of fish and, if they know of a secluded lake where there are large specimen fish to be caught, they will make every effort to fish there.

The third group are those who prefer competitive fishing. Each angler draws lots for a position or 'peg' on the bank. A whistle is then blown and all fish caught, regardless of size, are put into a keep-net. At the end of the day another whistle is blown and the contents of each keep-net is weighed. The angler with the greatest weight of fish wins the prize which, in the large competitions, can amount to a considerable sum. There is no doubt that professionalism is creeping in slowly but surely into a sport which was once the quiet hobby of country folk. Izaak Walton would surely be most intrigued if he could see anglers using catapults to project their ground-bait to a particular spot and all the expensive equipment which they nowadays employ.

A lake owner intending to use the resource for profit must decide which type of angler is to be catered for, because on this determines the type of fish introduced into the water. Also whether a large number of fish of medium size or a smaller number of greater size should be stocked. The best course would be to consult the local Fisheries Officer who may be able to supply the fish and who will, knowing the local conditions, be able to advise on the number and type of fish to be put in.

If the owner of a private lake decides to let the coarse fishing rights to an angling club, the water must be well stocked and large enough to provide for fifty or more fishing 'pegs' for a normal size match. In a newly-made lake, it means waiting perhaps two years for the stock to breed and become well established. After five years or so, it may be found that there are too many fish for the lake to support, causing a general stunting of growth. The owner will then have to have the stock reduced by electric stunning and netting out or by introducing a few pike. The lake owner should issue his own set of rules to the angling club with particular emphasis on leaving the bank tidy and not damaging vegetation.

Most angling clubs have strict rules about rubbish disposal and leaving bits of nylon on the bank. Throwing bits of nylon with lead weights attached into the water must be strictly forbidden. The lead weights get caught in the weeds which are eaten by swans, resulting in slow, prolonged death of the swan by lead poisoning. Nylon also gets tangled round the feet of waterfowl causing death by starvation. Inevitably, when a big fish breaks a weighted line, some lead is left in the water, but the tendency of some anglers, at the end of a day's fishing, to throw unwanted bits of nylon, with lead weights attached, into the water, must be discouraged.

There are various rules in different countries about keeping the fish that are caught. In the U K coarse fish are mostly returned to the water, but in most European countries the fish are often kept. However, minimum sizes exist for retention of edible fish such as pike.

If the lake is leased to non-competitive anglers who fish for the pleasure of catching specimen fish, the initial stock should contain some 1kg fish such as carp or tench which can be supplied by a fish farm. If pike are introduced, it will be necessary to put in perch, roach or rudd for the pike to feed on. Thereafter, there should be no need to introduce more fish for a considerable time.

The decision as to whether to lease a lake for trout fishing or for coarse fishing depends on a number of factors.

If, for example, a lake is set in a very pleasant environment in the middle of the country and is not easily accessible from the nearest town, then it would probably be more profitable and would involve much less invasion of privacy, if the lake was used as a trout fishery. But if someone has converted an old gravel pit into a fishing water, not far from a large town, then the wisest thing to do would be to use it for coarse fishing. The owner could either lease it to an angling club on the same terms as for trout fishing or he could let it out on a day-ticket basis, which would require someone permanently present to issue tickets and give general supervision. Such a lake would need to be accessible to a road and to have an adequate car park and toilet facilities. On no account should powerboats for water skiing be allowed on a lake which is used for serious fishing.

Crayfish

Many rivers and lakes with stoney bottoms used to contain the native crayfish (*Astacus astacus*) but most of this species have now been eliminated by a crayfish plague, a form of fungal disease. However, a new species of crayfish (*Pacifastacus leniusculus*), originally brought from America, has been cultivated in Sweden. This species is plague-resistant and grows faster and bigger than the native species.

There is a ready market for crayfish, particularly in France and Sweden, and anyone having a suitable pond or stream where native crayfish have been known to have been found in good numbers, might well consider stocking them. Crayfish require clear, well-oxygenated water, with a pH above 6. They like a stoney bottom where there are plenty of cracks and crevices in which to hide. If the bottom is silty, it can be remedied to some extent by removing as much silt as possible and replacing it with brick rubble and broken drainage pipes. Crayfish prefer the shallower water along the banks of lakes and streams where the water is warmer.

Unfortunately, the crayfish, from the time it is hatched till it is fully grown, has many enemies. Newly-hatched young are readily eaten by eels, fish, waterfowl and herons. Mink will take a heavy toll of them as they grow larger. It would seem, therefore, that unless crayfish can be reared under controlled and somewhat artificial conditions, or where the natural conditions are ideal, the chances of many of them reaching maturity would be small.

Young crayfish, only 10mm long, are expensive. To introduce them into waters of unknown suitability might involve considerable financial risk, especially as it is recommended that, to get the best results, stocking must be done for five successive years and only after a minimum of three years are the adults big enough to be caught in traps and marketed.

Anyone who is considering introducing crayfish to a lake should seek specialist advice on the suitability of the water and other details before making any capital outlay.

Rough shooting

Despite strong disapproval in some quarters there is an increasing demand for rough shooting and it is no longer the sport of the privileged few. A farmer who owns the shooting rights on a 500-acre (124ha) farm which has good hedges, perhaps a small wood and a moderately-sized lake, is likely to have a fair amount of mixed game on it. The advantage of having a lake in a shoot is that the common pheasant, being a bird of marsh and scrubland, is naturally attracted to rough cover near lakes and rivers and such a habitat will always draw pheasants, woodcock, wildfowl, quail and, in the U S A, even wild turkeys.

If a farmer owns the land surrounding a lake and grows a 25m wide strip of lucerne, kale or roots near the lake, leaving permanent rough grass round the boundaries, it will be an added attraction because this is the type of feeding ground pheasants like and, with a modicum of corn dispersed during winter weather, there will always be a nucleus of pheasants which will justify asking a high price for the shooting rights.

A sunny dry bank, free of weeds, is often much appreciated by birds who like sunbathing and dusting. Partridges, pheasants, and other game birds will welcome such a place where they can dry out their broods if they get wet in long grass. The best way to make a weed-free area is to have a large bonfire which will sterilize the soil and give good dusting material for a considerable time.

Shooting rights over such land could easily be let to four or five persons on a long-term lease with an annual review of the price. A long lease is much more likely to make the tenants do their own gamekeeping and preserve a breeding stock, whereas with a short-term lease, the tenants are apt to take everything they can. Nevertheless, the owner should specify a certain number of shooting days each season.

Duck shooting

There are very few open stretches of water in the world which are not visited by wild duck at one time or another. In the autumn ducks and other wildfowl migrate to the south, keeping to well-established migration routes. In North America they fly down the western and eastern coasts to South America. From northern Europe some fly down the Atlantic seaboard to West Africa or across Europe to East Africa. On all these journeys they are apt to be shot at by wildfowlers, but fortunately indiscriminate shooting is less common than it was and wholesale slaughter with a punt gun is no longer allowed. Limited shooting of the common species such as mallard (*Anas platyrhynchos*), teal (*Anas crecca*), wigeon (*Anas penelope*) does not appear to have any effect on their numbers.

Ducks spend most of the day sitting on the water's edge, sleeping or preening. At dusk they fly off to feed in meadows or stubbles and return in the morning. They feed mainly on seeds, shoots of water weed, small insects and worms and like feeding in shallow, flooded meadows where they can find numerous worms. If such places exist along the side of a lake, they should not be drained. Food, in the form of wheat or maize, will be readily eaten by ducks and should be put in water about 10cm deep, otherwise crows will take it. Ducks, with their sensitive beaks, will soon find it, even if it is covered with mud.

Wild ducks are, on the whole, very unsuccessful breeders. They start nesting early before there is much ground cover and very little lake-side vegetation, and though ten ducklings may be hatched off, they soon succumb to cold weather or fall prey to gulls, crows, magpies and ground vermin and few, if any, of the first brood survive. A second brood, a month or so later, when there is thicker cover about, may be more successful with perhaps a 30% survival rate. The female duck may well be responsible for the loss of some of her brood because she pays very little attention to stragglers which, once isolated from the brood, are killed by predators or perish from exposure.

If a lake is to be largely used for shooting purposes, reeds must be allowed to grow more freely round the margins and shallow, muddy patches, planted with watercress and duckweed, should be created. Ducks naturally prefer to nest on an island where they are fairly safe from all but aerial predators and the more islands the better. Such islands could be planted with brambles that will eventually grow well out over the water, providing excellent cover underneath for newly-hatched ducklings.

Artificially-reared mallard are sometimes put on to lakes during the late summer. They have to be penned and fed by the lake-side with full protection against marauding foxes and they become very tame. When the time comes for them to be shot at, it is often exceedingly difficult to get them to fly very far or very high and as each duck tries to get back to the lake, it is subjected to a fearful crossfire which is not only highly dangerous shooting but in no way can it be called sport. If artificially-reared duck are gradually permitted to fend for themselves and are not shot at during their first season, they soon lose their tameness through contact with visiting wild duck and, though they may fly off elsewhere, quite a number will return to breed each year if the environment proves suitable. In this way, a nucleus of breeding duck can be established, provided they are not decimated by excessive shooting.

A lake as a conservation area

In contrast to the use of a lake to provide sport, without doubt there are people who, if they owned a fair-sized lake, would prefer to put it to use as a wildlife sanctuary, particularly for birds whose natural habitat is being destroyed much more rapidly than that of other wild creatures. Our urban sprawl offers an excellent location for sparrows, starlings, foxes and grey squirrels but for little else; our tree-nesting birds, including most of the songsters, will soon experience great difficulty in finding somewhere safe to breed. The ruthless cutting of road hedges during the breeding season plus the complete removal of hedges, are only two examples of the serious inroads being made into the natural environment of wild birds. Some thousands of ornamental trees are planted each year in urban districts for decorative purposes but most of them, from the bird's viewpoint, are useless; so too are the dense forests of fir and spruce planted for timber.

Birds have four main requirements in life:

1. A reliable food supply
2. A safe place to breed
3. A safe roosting place
4. Freedom from persecution

If these four requirements can be found in one place, birds will soon appear and will stay to breed, with a good survival rate for the young.

Food

A lake and its surrounding area is an especially good place for bird conservation because insect life is always more abundant where there is a constant water supply, and is most plentiful just at the time when birds are feeding their young. During periods of drought, soft-billed birds, such as the thrush family (Turdidae), are unable to dig for worms and insects but round a lake there are usually damp patches where they can find what they want. A readily available water supply is an obvious advantage to birds of every variety.

Winter usually presents a food problem for birds and though most birds build up a store of fat in the autumn, this is soon used up on a prolonged spell of cold weather. Much can be done by planting the type of tree which produces berries the birds can eat during times of severe cold and such food may make the difference between life and death.

The common hawthorn (*Crataegus monogyna*) is perhaps the greatest stand-by for the thrush family, namely the mistlethrush (*Turdus viscivorus*), the song thrush (*Turdus musicus*), the redwing (*Turdus iliacus*), the fieldfare (*Turdus pilaris*), the blackbird (*Turdus merula*) and the ring ousel (*Turdus torquatus*). In most years hawthorn produces a fair crop of berries. A good berry year indicates that the previous spring was a favourable one for the setting of fruit and in no way forecasts a cold winter as is a popular belief. Much superstition attaches to the hawthorn tree and to cut one down is supposed to invite disaster.

Other winter berries, very valuable as a winter food for birds, are those of the firethorn (*Pyracantha coccinea*), the yew (*Taxus baccata*). the dog rose (*Rosa canina*), the rowan (*Sorbus aucuparia*), the swedish whitebeam (*Sorbus intermedia*) and the holly (*Ilex aquifolium*).

Trees which produce berries in the summer and autumn are also important especially in times of drought when soft billed birds cannot dig. Wild cherry (*Prunus avium*) and bird cherry (*Prunus padus*), elder (*Sambucus nigra*), blackberry (*Rubus fruticosus*), raspberry (*Rubus idaeus*), honeysuckle (*Lonicera periclymenum*) and cotoneaster (*Cotoneaster frigidus*) all produce berries which are eagerly taken by birds.

The common hazel (*Corylus avellana*) will always attract various species of woodpeckers (Picidae), nuthatches (Sittidae), and tits (Paridae), as it will the less desirable grey squirrel (*Sciurus carolinensis*). The beech (*Fagus sylvatica*) produces a very useful winter food for many birds. Pheasants are particularly fond of beech-mast. Many seed-eating finches also eat them. One of the most useful trees from the birds' point of view is the oak (*Quercus robur*) which, throughout the summer months, always has an abundance of insect life within its foliage on which the smaller insectivorous birds can feed their young.

Acorns will certainly attract pigeons (*Columba palumbus*) which are generally regarded by farmers as a pest; but it is better that pigeons eat acorns and keep away from the farmer's seed corn or brussel sprouts. Jays (*Garrulus glandarius*) are very fond of acorns, many of which they bury for future consumption. It is a pity that such attractive birds take the eggs and nestlings of any bird unable to defend itself but it is unlikely that there will be more than one pair of jays in a wood or zone because they drive off neighbouring jays which would readily take the eggs or nestlings of their own kind.

Other useful deciduous trees in a conservation area are the silver birch (*Betula pendula*) and the alder (*Alnus glutinosa*). Both trees provide seeds during the winter for parties of siskins (*Spinus spinus*), redpolls (*Acanthius linaria*), chaffinches (*Fringilla coelebs*) and most of the tit family. Woodpeckers frequently choose an alder or birch tree in which to dig out their nest holes. There are many common, large deciduous trees which are of little value to birds because they provide neither food nor shelter in the winter months and insufficient cover for nesting birds during the summer. The ash (*Fraxinus excelsior*) is an example. Another example is the sycamore (*Acer pseudoplatanus*) which is the largest of European maples and often grows to a height of 30m, occupying a lot of space. Other members of the decorative acer family are unfortunately of little use for birds. Likewise all the poplar family are of little value and will quickly occupy a lot of space, cutting off light to the ground below, thereby preventing the growth of useful vegetation and small shrubs. Willows have been previously mentioned and they too come into the same category unless they are kept pollarded when they can form most useful nesting sites, mainly for hole-nesting birds.

Nesting and roosting places
Evergreen trees and shrubs are of vital importance to all forms of wildlife, providing protection from the weather and from predators such as birds of prey. They provide roosting and nesting sites for birds and ground cover for animals.

The best evergreen is probably the common rhododendron (*Rhododendron ponticum*) which in the last century was often planted in woods to give cover for pheasants. The bushes should be planted to form thick clumps, about 30m by 30m. When fully grown, they will keep the ground underneath almost free of frost and snow, thus providing a feeding ground for birds and animals and a great protection against wind, which most birds dislike intensely. Other very useful evergreens are laurel (*Prunus laurocerasus*), holly (*Ilex aquifolium*), yew (*Taxus baccata*), holm oak (*Quercus ilex*) and ivy (*Hedera helix*).

Care must be taken about planting cypress and fir trees, some of which will soon grow to a great height and will only be useful for less desirable species such as crows and pigeons. The aim is to obtain trees which are of slow growth and have a compact foliage. There are now many hybrids of Leyland and Lawson cypress which are suitable and very attractive in shape. Small birds use such trees for roosting and nesting and as places where they can hide if a winged predator is nearby.

Dead trees, though they may present an unsightly appearance, should not be cut down unless dangerous, because they provide an excellent feeding ground for woodpeckers, tree creepers (*Certhiidae*), tits and nuthatches and they may have holes in which owls will nest and bats may often have a colony. Ivy-covered trees are very important for roosting birds and should be encouraged. There is a popular belief that ivy will kill a tree by 'sucking the goodness' out of it: this is not so, the ivy merely uses the tree as a support.

The best habitat for small birds would be one where trees and shrubs are planted in small groups, leaving open spaces in between into which light can penetrate and allow ground cover such as brambles, nettles, thistles, wild flowers and weeds to grow. Open spaces, in light woodland, make an excellent habitat for many varieties of butterfly whose breeding places are becoming progressively scarcer, due to the wide use of weedkillers.

The lake itself could be said to be the nucleus of the conservation area and, if undisturbed by regular fishing, water skiing or other noisy activities, will certainly attract birds that live on or near water.

Sedge can be allowed to grow more freely but the usual precautions must be taken to keep the lake-weed under reasonable control.

Such a habitat is ideal for some of the many species of warblers (Sylviidae) and where there are warblers there are usually cuckoos (Cuculidae). Kingfishers (Alcedinidae) will probably take up residence if there is a good supply of small fish in the lake and will breed if they can find a suitable bank. Grebes (Podicipitidae) are sure to appear and breed if the lake is undisturbed. Many other species will be attracted because birds can get a much easier living near water where there is usually a plentiful supply of insects upon which to feed themselves and their young.

It is advisable to have a length of shoreline which is weed-free and shallow where birds and animals can drink and bathe. This will attract ducks, waders and wagtails (Motacillidae) amongst others. As a place for observation or photography it is ideal because in hot weather there is usually a steady stream of birds coming down for a drink and quite often a rare species appears suddenly.

As regards stocking with fish, any variety of coarse fish, including minnows and sticklebacks, can be put in for the benefit of fish-eating birds and if the owner himself wants to fish, he can add a few trout or even carp, but not pike as these will readily take small waterfowl.

Nesting boxes

There is little doubt that the population of small birds which nest in cavities can be considerably increased by the provision of suitable nest boxes.

Some species of tits like a closed box with an entrance hole about 3cm in diameter, robins (*Erithacus rubecula*) like an open-fronted box well concealed in ivy. Spotted flycatchers (*Muscicapa striata*) will choose an open-fronted box often in an exposed position (*Fig 54*). Such a box, fixed on the wall of a boat-house in a creeper, will often be used as a nesting site by wagtails.

Wrens may use an ordinary tit box in the winter months as a communal roost, rather than for nesting, and as many as 30 or 40 wrens will roost there, packing themselves in to conserve body heat. Invariably they choose a box that has been well constructed, draught proof and watertight and there is little doubt that such boxes greatly reduce their winter mortality.

Boxes must be fixed firmly to tree trunks or posts about 2m above ground but the nails must not be driven in completely so that the box can be removed for cleaning out. Where possible, it should be fixed on the underslope of a tree to make it more difficult for climbing predators to get at the box.

If there are no well-established trees, poles can be used for nestboxes. A creeper such as Russian ivy (*Polygonum*) can be trained up them. This creeper has a very attractive feathery flower in the autumn and grows at such a prodigious rate that a pole can be completely covered by a season's growth, making excellent cover for small birds.

Fig 54 An open nest box and ordinary tit boxes are safer from predators if fixed on the under-slope of a tree trunk

The question may be asked: 'Why bother to provide nest boxes and appliances? Surely there are enough natural nesting sites for cavity-nesting birds?' The answer is that old trees, often with many holes and hollows in them, are nowadays cut down with modern power saws all too soon and disposed of very rapidly; old brick buildings and stone walls, with many a nook and crany, are bulldozed away and replaced by concrete and barbed wire. As a result there is often fierce competition and fighting for nesting sites in the spring, the larger and usually more common birds being the victors.

Animal life and predators

Wherever there is abundance of bird life, there is certain to be plenty of animal life, too. Animals such as foxes, stoats and badgers who, before the days of myxomatosis in Europe and the U K relied largely on young rabbits for their livelihood, have been forced to change their diet to include the eggs and young of birds nesting on or near the ground and also dead or weak adult birds, as might be found below a roost. Foxes are unexpectedly good climbers; stoats and weasels even more so, but these animals are all part of the natural ecology killing, as they do, many rats and mice which attack birds nesting on or near the ground and they

129

should therefore be left entirely alone.

Feral cats are very likely to be found in a conservation area. These unfortunate animals, who have been forced to take to the wild because their owners would not feed them, are often in poor condition, resulting from what is for them a rough and hostile environment. But some become very successful killers and breed. They usually hunt at night and can cause panic if they get into a large roost of birds. The best thing to do is to obtain a trap specially made for this purpose and bait it with liver. When caught, the unfortunate creature should be destroyed by a veterinary surgeon.

Almost none of our smaller birds are safe from the grey squirrel during the nesting season; even those which nest in boxes or tree holes are often attacked and made to desert their nests. Some of our public parks would make excellent bird sanctuaries, were it not for its presence.

Another unwelcome visitor would be mink which, if allowed free rein, would soon disturb the whole life of the waterfowl and lake-side birds. If anyone reports having seen an otter in the district the presence of a mink must be suspected, especially if it is in a mink area, and a search must be made for tell-tale signs of its presence and, if necessary, action taken as described in *Chapter 5*.

Hawks, falcons and other birds of prey must be encouraged. Our smaller birds, over thousands of years, have developed an instinctive fear of hawks and have adapted themselves to take rapid, and usually successful, evasive action. Small birds seem to have an advanced warning system. This is seen when the sudden appearance of a hunting hawk, dashing through a woodland, causes an immediate and absolute silence and the temporary disappearance into thick cover of all bird life except, perhaps, for a weak bird which is quickly seized.

Too many magpies (*Pica pica*), carrion crows (*Corus corone corone*) and jays are very unwelcome visitors when birds are nesting. They will search out and devour eggs and nestlings.

In the days when the larger hawks and falcons were common in every country, these thieving birds were kept under control. Only the smaller hawks and falcons have survived man's onslaught and these are too small to tackle birds the size of a magpie, crow or jay, and the latter, always quick to learn, have have moved into suburban gardens where they have no enemies and a good food supply; in winter they even take food from bird tables. The result is that their numbers are rapidly increasing which is bad for smaller birds.

Human interference

In general, provided wild birds and animals are not interfered with by man upsetting their environment, they are quite able to look after themselves. They have amazing powers of recovery from the natural extremes of weather which occur from time to time and, given a few favourable breeding seasons, their numbers get back to normal. But the persistent pressure put on them by man in the form of removal of their natural environment, pollution, herbicides, road deaths and the all too frequent invasion of the few remaining quiet places in the countryside made possible by the motorcar, is something with which wild life cannot cope and the numbers of more interesting species will begin to drop.

Bird-watching and bird photography are becoming more and more popular. To many members of the public, a bird is now no longer just a bird, but an individual species and this new interest is greatly to be encouraged and is proving invaluable for the preservation of some of our rarer birds. But a word of warning must be given. There are many over-enthusiastic, amateur bird-watchers and photographers who inadvertently disturb birds at a critical period of their nesting activities and, by prolonged presence near their nests, may cause them to forsake their eggs. Nesting birds need as much privacy as possible: they have enough worries in the form of wild predators without the interference of man. Great care should therefore be taken by would-be ornithologists that only the minimal disturbance is caused.

Urban sprawl is the biggest threat to our less common birds and animals, because it takes away and does not replace their natural habitat. Open ditches and ponds are filled in, marsh land is drained and common land, often covered with massive clumps of blackberry bushes and other thick scrub, is 'tidied up' by a bulldozer and made into playing fields. But it is by no means all gloom as far as birds are concerned.

About a century ago, the attitude towards wildlife was that it was there to be exploited and the word conservation hardly existed. The U S A were the first by a long way to realize the necessity of establishing conservation areas – Yellowstone National Park was started in 1872, Lake Merritt in 1970 and Pelican Island in 1903.

Since then other countries have followed suit and there are now many sanctuaries in the U K, France, Germany, Poland, the U S S R, Finland, Sweden, Holland, Austria, Italy, Japan, Asia and Australasia. Ornithological societies have been formed in these countries and are largely responsible for the establishment of these sanctuaries. The well-known Audubon Society was formed in the U S A in 1886. It is strongly supported everywhere in the U S A and represents a powerful body of opinion. The Royal Society for Protection of Birds was founded in the U K soon afterwards, in 1889.

Most societies have been able to establish some degree of legal protection of birds in their countries, which is a good start, but law enforcement is not easy. One big step in the right direction is that public opinion, from being somewhat indifferent to the idea of conservation, is now very much in favour of it. A great deal of the credit for this must go to the excellent wildlife films displayed on television; these are not only very interesting to both young and old but are especially helpful in altering childrens' attitudes to birds and animals, which is often somewhat aggressive due more to lack of understanding than to anything else.

There is still a vast amount to be done to preserve wildlife but it is fair to say that the tide of indiscriminate destruction has begun to turn. Anyone owning a country property, a farm or even a town garden can help by creating small nature reserves on the lines suggested, but they must not expect too much too soon. If birds could read notices it would be easier but they establish themselves by trial and usage rather than anything else and if the habitat is to their liking they will stay around. If they are migrants they may return each year to breed but if the environment is not suitable, they will look elsewhere.

References

Better Angling with Simple Science: Mary Pratt – Fishing News Books Ltd, Farnham, Surrey, U K.

British Freshwater Fishes: M E Varley – Fishing News Books Ltd, Farnham, Surrey, U K.

Collins Guide to Freshwater Fishes of Britain and Europe: Bent J Muus and Preben Dahlstrom – Collins, London.

Crayfish – K J Richards, Riversdale Farm, Stour Provost, Dorset, U K.

Earth Ponds: Tim Matson – Countryman Press, Woodstock, Vermont, U S A.

European Inland Water Fish – A multilingual catalogue: Food and Agriculture Organization of the U N – Fishing News Books Ltd, Farnham, Surrey, U K.

Field Guide to Birds of Britain: Reader's Digest Association, London : New York : Montreal : Sydney.

Fish Farmer – Agricultural Press, Sutton, Surrey.

Fishing with electricity: Food and Agriculture Organization of the U N – Fishing News Books Ltd, Farnham, Surrey, U K.

Handbook of Trout and Salmon Diseases: R J Roberts and C J Shepherd – Fishing News Books Ltd, Farnham, Surrey, U K.

Loch Fishing: R C Bridgett – Herbert Jenkins, London.

Ministry of Agriculture and Fisheries Publications Branch, Pinner, Middlesex, U K.
  Control of aquatic weed Bulletin 194 –
  Dam construction –
  Farm water supply Bulletin 2 –
  Water for irrigation Bulletin 202 –

Observer's Book of Pond Life: John Clegg – Frederick Warne, New York : London.

Textbook of Fish Culture: Marcel Huet – Fishing News Books Ltd, Farnham, Surrey, U K.

The Creation of Low-cost Fisheries – Angling Foundation, London.

The Trout: W E Frost and M E Brown – Collins, London.

Trout Farming Manual: J P Stevenson – Fishing News Books Ltd, Farnham, Surrey, U K.

Trout Flies: C F Walker – Herbert Jenkins, London.

Two Lakes: Alex Behrendt – André Deutsch, London.

Conversion Table

1 kilogram	=	2.205 lbs.
1 lb	=	0.454 kg.
		(or 454.0 gms.)
30.5 cm	=	1 foot (12 inches)
1 metre	=	100 cm.
		or 3.28 ft.
1 hectare	=	100 ares
		or 2.471 acres.
1 acre	=	0.405 hectare
		or 4,840 square yards
10 acres	=	4.05 hectares
1 gallon	=	4.546 litres.

Other books published by
Fishing News Books Ltd

Free catalogue available on request

Advances in aquaculture
Advances in fish science and technology
Aquaculture practices in Taiwan
Atlantic salmon: its future
Better angling with simple science
British freshwater fishes
Commercial fishing methods
Control of fish quality
Culture of bivalve molluscs
Echo sounding and sonar for fishing
The edible crab and its fishery in
    British waters
Eel capture, culture, processing and
    marketing
Eel culture
Engineering, economics and
    fisheries management
European inland water fish: a multilingual
    catalogue
FAO catalogue of fishing gear designs
FAO catalogue of small scale fishing gear
FAO investigates ferro-cement fishing craft
Farming the edge of the sea
Fish and shellfish farming in coastal waters
Fish catching methods of the world
Fisheries of Australia
Fisheries oceanography and ecology
Fisheries sonar
Fishermen's handbook
Fishery products
Fishing boats and their equipment
Fishing boats of the world 1
Fishing boats of the world 2
Fishing boats of the world 3
The fishing cadet's handbook
Fishing ports and markets
Fishing with electricity
Fishing with light
Freezing and irradiation of fish
Glossary of UK fishing gear terms
Handbook of trout and salmon diseases
Handy medical guide for seafarers

How to make and set nets
Inshore fishing: its skills, risks,rewards
Introduction to fishery by-products
The lemon sole
A living from lobsters
Marine fisheries ecosystem
Marine pollution and sea life
Marketing in fisheries and aquaculture
The marketing of shellfish
Mending of fishing nets
Modern deep sea trawling gear
Modern fishing gear of the world 1
Modern fishing gear of the world 2
Modern fishing gear of the world 3
More Scottish fishing craft and their work
Multilingual dictionary of fish and
    fish products
Navigation primer for fishermen
Netting materials for fishing gear
Pair trawling and pair seining
Pelagic and semi-pelagic trawling gear
Planning of aquaculture development
Power transmission and automation
    for ships and submersibles
Refrigeration on fishing vessels
Salmon and trout farming in Norway
Salmon fisheries of Scotland
Scallop and queen fisheries of the
    British Isles
Scallops and the diver-fisherman
Seafood fishing for amateur and
    professional
Seine fishing
Squid jigging from small boats
Stability and trim of fishing vessels
The stern trawler
Study of the sea
Textbook of fish culture
Training fishermen at sea
Trends in fish utilization
Trout farming manual
Tuna: distribution and migration
Tuna fishing with pole and line